The Mediation Handbook
2014/15

The Mediation Handbook 2014/15

2nd Edition

Jonathan Dingle and Judith Kelbie

UNITY PRESS

Contents

Chapters

Appendices

Acknowledgements

With thanks to: Ian Strathcarron, Lizzie Haynes, Marguerite Wilcox, and the LSM Faculty including John Harvey, Zoey White, Michelle Baines, John Sephton, Steve Malcolm OBE

and the inspirational mediation cartoonist Charles Pugsley Fincher J.D.

Dedication to the first Mediation Handbook

When we were asked by colleagues and friends to write the Mediation Handbook, we were immediately humbled and daunted. Mediation has been so important to us for so many years, and there have been so many inspiring people we have met in the profession and in academia, we realised we had so many colleagues to thank before we could even sit down and begin.

Mediation was introduced to Jonathan at a community centre in Catford in the late 1970s at a time when only *The Smurfs* and dog track lovers knew of the little South London district. Yet watching conciliators in action made a very strong impression on him that has lasted a professional lifetime. Judith trained with Stitt, Feld and Handy in London more than a decade ago and was at once seized by the *Notre Dame University* skills they presented. The passion for mediation was aroused and led her into a completely new professional direction.

For both though, there is one figure in this country who stands out as a beacon in making mediation central to their commitment to change: Sir Brian Neill. SBN, as he is affectionately known to one and all, after an incisive career as a judge, founded the Civil Mediation Council and then put it into an order that fellow giants, the late Lord Gordon Slynn and the wonderful Sir Henry Brooke could carry forward.

Sir Brian continues to do his all – he thinks little of travelling to Manchester to preside at a mediation competition between Manchester and Liverpool Universities, however long the journey and demanding the students. He crosses countries making the world a better place in so many ways.

It is therefore to him that we dedicate the Mediation Handbook, and offer our own sincere thanks for all his support, motivation, wisdom and energy. We are sure that these sentiments are echoed in every quarter of the mediation community.

Jonathan and Judith

London, 1st January 2013

Foreword to the 2014/15 Edition

We are delighted to offer this, the second edition of The Mediation Handbook. More than 12,000 copies of the first 2013/14 edition were downloaded despite its flaws, typos and enthusiasts' errors, which we believe made it one of the largest selling mediation books of all time. This edition follows up with a more succinct and directed text and better index, organisation and clarity.

For that we are indebted to Ian Strathcarron, our editor, fellow mediator and friend who has put in many hours of devoted and myopia-inducing effort to make the book readable. The result is clear to see. The mistakes and misconceptions remain the authors but huge credit and thanks go to Ian and the team at Unity Press, who, like good mediators have listened, listened, listened and not made matters worse.

Jonathan and Judith

London, 20th February 2014

Introduction

In January 2010, in his report on civil litigation costs[1] Sir Rupert Jackson wrote:

> In my view there now needs to be a single authoritative handbook, explaining clearly and concisely what Alternative Dispute Resolution (ADR) is (without either hype nor jargon) and giving details of all reputable providers of mediation… The obvious utility of such a work means that it would be self-financing. It needs to have a highly respected editor, perhaps a recently retired senior judge. It needs to become the vade mecum of every judge or lawyer dealing with mediation issues. It should be the textbook used in every Judicial Studies Board (JSB) seminar or Continuing Professional Development (CPD) training session. I am not proposing any formal system of accreditation, although that would be an option. However, inclusion of any mediation scheme or organisation in this handbook will be a mark of respectability. The sort of handbook which I have in mind will be a work of equivalent status to the annual publications about civil procedure. Most judges and litigators would have the current edition of the proposed handbook on their bookshelves.

Three years elapsed after those wise words before the Civil Justice Council[2] (CJC) and the Civil Mediation Council[3] (CMC) published an ADR guide, which followed the first edition of the Mediation Handbook. The two books cover very different ground and the authors of this book, two internationally recognised mediation trainers[4] with a combined 14 years service as board members of the CMC, have written this second edition in association with the London School of Mediation, 218 Strand Chambers, *Specialist Info*, and 7 Solicitors LLP.

Sir Rupert Jackson recognised that mediation, as a leading form of ADR, is an increasingly promoted solution to rising costs, delays, and procedural satellite litigation associated with all manner of claims and disputes worldwide. Indeed since he published the report all indications suggest that the practice of mediation has more than doubled across all sectors where it could be used.

This book therefore aims to provide both the lawyer and the layman[5] with a good understanding of the forms of mediation, to set out a short history of the use of the process, to illustrate the contemporary approach of the English courts, and to provide a practical guide to using mediation. In doing so, it provides guidance for identifying cases which may, and may not, be candidates for mediation as opposed to more traditional forms of dispute

---

[1] http://www.judiciary.gov.uk/NR/rdonlyres/8EB9F3F3-9C4A-4139-8A93-56F09672EB6A/0/jacksonfinalreport140110.pdf Chapter 38 paragraph 3.8
[2] http://www.judiciary.gov.uk/about-the-judiciary/advisory-bodies/cjc
[3] http://www.civilmediation.org/
[4] See Appendix 9 and http://www.schoolofmediation.org
[5] 'Layman' is used throughout the handbook to avoid using the clumsy 'layperson', although layperson is its meaning.

resolution. These forms range across the spectrum from early and co-operative negotiation to vigorously contested litigation. The latter is becoming less common: with the England and Wales reforms of April 2013 it already seems that fewer than 1% of issued cases will be decided in court, with the remainder being settled out of court – or abandoned. The UK Government is committed to participating in mediation or other forms of ADR wherever possible.

Litigation and telephone negotiations retain their places in the toolkit: not every case needs, warrants, or justifies the use of a mediator. It is as important to recognise, as the present chair of the Civil Justice Council (CJC) Lord Dyson said in his review of the watershed English case of *Halsey*[6], that mediation is not always a panacea in all cases – as it is to understand the real strengths and opportunities that the process offers.

The opportunities, in mediating civil, business, commercial, banking, financial, NHS, insurance, injury, trusts and funds disputes are substantial and becoming more so. This book addresses them realistically and the sample at Annex A offers an insight into the process and the role of the mediator.

This Handbook does, however, commend mediation and many are delighted that it is an increasingly natural part of society. It is hoped that the reader will come to regard this book as a *guide, philosopher, and friend*[7] and thereby gain or increase a passion for the process: and come to use or engage in it should circumstances permit.

The authors, for whom mediation is a passion, acknowledge the many who have contributed in different ways to the production of this Handbook. Without their help the Handbook would be a mere shadow of itself: the authors must however record that the responsibility for any errors and omissions, and judgment calls in assembling the text, is solely their own. They welcome corrections and ideas for the Third Edition due in Spring 2015.

Please do email jonathan@schoolofmediation.org or call them on 0207 427 0848.

---

[6] Halsey v-Milton Keynes General NHS Trust [2004] EWCA 3006 Civ 576 suggests that mediation or ADR should be used unless there are reasonable grounds for litigation. A failure to mediate could be reflected in costs. http://www.bailii.org/ew/cases/EWCA/Civ/2004/576.html
[7] As was said of the late Professor Glanville Williams' book "*Learning The Law*" (14 edns: 1945-2010)

Giraffe mediator breaks ice with lame joke.

Chapter 1: What is Mediation?

What it is

Mediation is a key form of Alternative Dispute Resolution (ADR). Alternative here means an alternative to having a decision imposed by a judge in court.

Mediation is a consensual process, based on self-determination that involves the participants in the dispute, together with their lawyers, advisers, or supporters, if they have any, meeting with a neutral third person. The mutual aim is to find a resolution to the dispute or problem that the participants face

It is a confidential and without prejudice activity that allows the participants to explore the full range of potential solutions in a safe environment. The neutral, or mediator, may encourage the use of principled negotiation, based upon reason and objective criteria. The mediator may reality-test the perceptions of fact, advantage, risk, and cost; and thereby assist the participants to find a mutually acceptable solution.

The solution need not be, and often is not, an outcome that a judge might or could properly impose through a decision in a court which is limited by legal constraints, rights, and precedents. It is simply the unique resolution found by the participants in the mediation that is 'good enough' for them in all the circumstances. The resolution is often more comprehensive and creative than a judgment or an arbitral award. It can provide a "win-win" outcome for the participants. As part of the search for a solution a skilled mediator will often look for added value which is often missed in mainstream negotiations, but can be a way of removing deadlock.

Mediation is therefore generally forward-focussed, not backward-looking. The past cannot be changed, but it can sometimes be cathartic to explore and rebuild relationships where this is an important step in securing a resolution. This transformative approach features in some family, community, and workplace cases, but it is not the central theme of most civil and commercial mediation. There, more commonly, the mediation will look to build a solution that works and will be durable.

What it is not

Mediation does not involve the mediator telling the participants the solution - or even venturing suggestions. It is for the participants themselves to find, with the mediator's assistance, and to agree a solution that meets their needs, concerns, and interests. Control remains with the participants. It does not involve the mediator telling the participants what a judge may or will do, or who is right or wrong. Nor does it involve the mediator assessing the merits of the case: after all, the mediator may not be aware of all of the relevant information, or even the relevant law. Mediators are commonly not lawyers and, because participants generally bring their own advisors, mediators do not need to be experts in the legal context of the dispute.

Misconceptions

There are many misconceptions of the role of the mediator, which may hinder participants agreeing to mediate. Those commonly encountered are:

- Mediation requires compromise from one or both participants – it does not: very often the outcome is unexpected and allows both to grow.

- The mediator is an evaluator – there should be no evaluation by a mediator: any assessment of risk or merits is for the participants.

- The mediator is an arbitrator - arbitration is a wholly different statute-based process involving legal assessment by, in effect, a private judge.

- The mediator will impose a solution – a mediator has no such power.

- The mediator will knock heads together – a mediator has no such role.

- The mediator will apply pressure on the participants – the only pressure that participants experience is that from their own assessment of risk.

- The mediator will advise the participants what to do – the participants must rely on their own judgment, or that of their advisers.

- Mediation is unlikely to be successful – around 90% of mediations result in a resolution on the day or shortly afterwards.

Oranges are not the only fruit

The concept of added value is demonstrated by the anecdote known as the mediator's orange. It has been fondly told to generations of training courses and begins with a mother going into the kitchen to find her two daughters arguing over the last orange in the fruit bowl. She intervenes, taking the fruit from the children and cutting it in half. Each daughter is given half the orange.

One daughter goes into the lounge and sits down to peel her half of the orange. She throws the peel in the bin and eats the fruit. The other daughter stays in the kitchen, carefully removes the peel from the fruit, throws the fruit away and uses the peel to bake a cake.

The knife represents the law: the equal division was a legal solution. But the outcome could have been very different had the mother asked: "Why do you want the orange?" Had she done so and each daughter answered honestly, then both could have had 100% more. The mother could have added value at no cost – with perhaps the chance to gain even better involvement with her hungry offspring.

It is a powerful if apocryphal story but one that illustrates the strength of the why questions so favoured by mediators: and often missed by negotiators.

A practical example

Away from fruit bowls and families, many people say that perhaps the most contentious disputes are those involving property boundaries. Whether they be around leylandii hedges or ransom strips, abandoned cars or fence lines, scraps between neighbours can quickly turn ugly and expensive.

From the casebook, comes a matter where neighbours had been in litigation for four years, over a less than a square foot of land. The significance for them was that without the seemingly innocuous patch, the local authority would not permit access for commercial vehicles to development fields due to width restrictions. Both neighbours engaged solicitors to provide legal advice and, by the date that mediation is arranged, each neighbour has spent enormous sums obtaining that advice and pursuing or defending the claim through the courts.

Both firms of solicitors, on the facts known to them, appeared strongly to embrace the view that their client was in the right. They appeared to have advised that their respective client had reasonable prospects of success in the litigation. Neither solicitor could guarantee that their client would win, however, and both agreed that the judicial outcome would be that one of the neighbours will be deemed to be the legal owner of the piece of land. There would be a winner and a loser. The loser would bear the winner's costs in addition to their own: in short, it would be a disaster for one of them.

The judge, as is the modern way in that Civil Justice Centre way, strongly recommended mediation. A month later the neighbours were in neutral offices. The mediator asked each of them, in private, why they wanted the land. One wanted the land in order to be able to develop the fields behind into the most profitable commercial site. Without it, planning consent would only be granted for a smaller scheme as the alternative access was not wide enough. The other wanted the land as his ownership would, he hoped, prevent any development, which might otherwise devalue their property. The lawyers have focussed on plans, maps, photographs, and an arboricultural consultant reports which aim to determine the line of the dividing wire fence which was entwined around the trunk of an old tree. There are numerous volumes of papers.

As mediation developed, the potential developer told the mediator in private that they have an alternate access route to the site but the scheme would be less profitable. It seemed that the development would go ahead in any event, but the developer would rather have access through the more direct route, which is the subject of the dispute.

The neighbour concerned about the devaluation of their property was unaware of the alternate access route and believed that they could stop the current planned development altogether. They had not understood that some development was inevitable in the short term but did recognise that something might happen one day.

It emerged that this neighbour do not intend to stay in the property to await that day and planned to move as soon as the dispute is resolved. Thus the mediator discovered (rather contrary to the impression created by the papers sent beforehand) that neither participant planned to stay in their premises in the future. There was not likely to be an ongoing relationship to salvage, simply an accord to be reached

The mediator asked how much a trial would cost and what each participant thought would happen. They both agreed that they might lose, and if they did, it would be very costly. The mediator explored potential solutions with them, and it dawned that the developer would be willing to make a premium payment in order to secure immediate ownership of the land. The neighbour was interested.

The question then turned on how much? The developer naturally wished to pay as little as possible, while the neighbour sought the greatest reward. A sticking point emerged some millions apart so the mediator again explored the alternatives to settlement, and involved the legal advisers in reality testing with their clients.

Through principled negotiation, using some objective criteria as to value and premium, a settlement was reached and an agreement drawn up by the lawyers. After months of conflict, and princely sums, the dispute was resolved amicably in four hours through intelligent, neutral, and private questioning.

More about mediation

Such outcomes are not new. Many outside the law, and in particular historians, are surprised that alternative dispute resolution processes have taken so long to come to the fore. Other civilisations embraced mediation long ago. There are references in Justinian, and before that historians speak of the Phoenicians using mediation in commercial disputes. In Greece a mediator was termed a προξηνητησ. In China there has been a long tradition of compromise and the works of Confucius suggest that he favoured persuasion rather than coercion. In Kerala, such a fusion of cultures, there is a similar history of negotiated settlement and appropriately the Indian Institute of Arbitration and Mediation[8] is based in Cochin. There are other traditions where a neutral third party has helped disputants reach an accord: the Quakers, as merely one example, have played a distinguished role.

But in the West, and despite the Abraham Lincoln enjoinder to discourage litigation: persuade your neighbours to compromise wherever you can, the practice until the 20th century was to use a third party judge in formal court proceedings or more recently an arbitrator or adjudicator, to determine a dispute – rather than to enlist a neutral to assist the disputants to reach a conclusion themselves. The process was adversarial.

Gradually, however, with the rising complexity of litigation, increasing delay, and the international nature of business, people began to question whether there might not be a more effective alternative to litigation. Conciliation procedures began to spring up in industrial relations, notably in the cotton industry and in 1896, the Conciliation Act was

---

[8] www.arbitrationindia.com

passed. Not long after in the USA the Department of Labor set up a panel of Commissioners of Conciliation to handle disputes.

It is generally recognised, however, that it was not until the last third or so of the 20th century that serious attention was given to the settlement of disputes by mediation. The early drivers towards mediation and ADR in the New World were not directly a response to the needs of clients for control or choice. The precipitators were rather the clogged court systems and prohibitive costs associated with traditional litigation.

It became fashionable to criticise the use of courts and their Victorian values when a more Aquarian option was developing.

ADR organisations in Canada, for example, emerged 20 or so years ago to become major clearing houses for litigation through combining the skills of forward thinking QC's, recently retired judges and ADR practitioners keen on promoting access to justice – with the demands of the insurance industry.

This cost-aware industry began effectively promoting the use of mediation in personal injury and clinical negligence claims to avoid leakage and reserve overruns.

Lawyers and clients were initially suspicious. Lawyers in particular felt threatened or discomforted by a process they did not understand. Some felt they may not be able to extract due rewards: or that reasonable expectations of profit costs may be thwarted. This was a factor identified in 1997[10] in the United Kingdom. There were over the next fifteen years, and remain reports of resistance to mediation in a number of countries which, on examination, appear to say more about the litigators involved, or their financial interests, than merits of the cases or the process. The UK Government, in contrast, came into mediation, however, with first the Government Pledge announced on 23rd March 2001 to embrace ADR and mediation, and then the *Dispute Resolution Commitment*[11] a decade later. The savings and effectiveness are reported and reviewed, and wide-ranging resources including the Small Claims Mediation Service[12] and (the now unfunded) *National Mediation Helpline* that have been used to promote mediation. Why?

Cost and speed are certainly factors attracting governments and individuals, organisations and litigants to mediation in this age of austerity. Privacy and confidentiality are others. But it is important to understand the scope of mediation and how it works.

---

[9] Notably Brian Wheatley QC and Glenn MacPherson QC at ADR Chambers
[10] See the reports of Dame Professor Hazel Genn CBE
[11] http://www.justice.gov.uk/courts/mediation/dispute-resolution-commitment
[12] http://www.justice.gov.uk/courts/mediation

The scope of mediation

Mediation is a voluntary process for resolving disputes by mutual agreement. It differs fundamentally from both arbitration and judicial determination at a trial in that no decision is, or can be, imposed by the mediator. Any settlement arising at mediation will be one which the participants own, and have created for themselves. The mediator is a midwife rather than a parent.

Mediation can be applied to all, or to just a discreet part, of a dispute. Brown and Marriott[13] observe that a dispute is a class or kind of conflict which manifests itself in a distinct, justiciable issue; a disagreement over issues capable of resolution by negotiation, mediation, or third party adjudication. Mediation offers an impartial, mutually acceptable and neutral guide to help disputing parties through the *tangled thicket of their conflict*[14] to a resolution of their own crafting.

In contrast to a trial, mediation is a private process, normally paid for by the participants, conducted at a time, at a place, and by a mediator of their choice. It follows the principles of self-determination and works under an ethical code.

Mediation: A legal or contractual process?

For now, at least, in the United Kingdom mediation is a contractual process. Spain (as from July 2012[15]), Austria (as from June 2003[16]), Ireland[17] and many other states have a mediation law, or court rules for mediation, but in the United Kingdom there are presently none. The Society of Mediators, a UK charity, is in 2013 addressing this under a voluntary Code of Practice but the law remains properly absent.

Lord Justice (Sir Rupert) Jackson did not recommend legislation and neither did the authors in their 2012 submissions to the Ministry of Justice: the view remains that mediation is a private process and not one in which the state needs to interfere. Thus, the participants will normally sign a Mediation Agreement with the mediator which defines the procedure and sets out what the participants and the mediator can and cannot do, before, at, and after the mediation. It is therefore not a creature of statute, but a contractual one and can exist entirely outside the current Civil Procedure Rules 1998 (CPR) which defines the legal

---

[13] *ADR: Principles and Practice* 3rd Edition 2011 (paperback 2012)
[14] Richard Weiler's expressive phrase
[15] http://www.boe.es/boe/dias/2012/03/06/pdfs/BOE-A-2012-3152.pdf
[16] http://portal.wko.at/wk/format_detail.wk?angid=1&stid=362257&dstid=0&titel=Austrian,Mediation,Act
[17] Order 56A of the Rules of the Superior Courts (Mediation and Conciliation) 2010

process. There are several advantages to mediation being a non-judicial process. It follows that because the process is voluntary, contractual, and independent of statutory restriction, the solutions which the parties decide to adopt do not need – in most cases – to have anything in common with the orders to which a court or arbitrator are restricted.

Apologies, explanations, meetings with consultants, amendments to policies, staff retraining, changes in procedures, therapy, counselling, admission for further or new treatments and second opinions are just some examples of highly creative solutions which mediations devise and which judges cannot aspire.

Mediation and English rules of court

Although there is neither proscription nor regulation, the CPR[18] does seek to encourage ADR, and so by implication mediation:

Rule 1.4(1) obliges the court to further the overriding objective of enabling the court to deal with cases justly by actively managing cases:

Rule 1.4(2)(e) defines active case management as including *encouraging the parties to use an alternative dispute resolution procedure if the court considers that appropriate and facilitating the use of such procedure.*

Rule 26.4(1) provides that *a party may, when filing the completed allocation questionnaire, make a written request for the proceedings to be stayed while the parties try to settle the case by alternative dispute resolution or other means.* The court/judiciary can also stay the case if considered appropriate.

Rule 44.5(3)(a)(ii) requires the court, in deciding the amount of costs to be awarded, to have regard to the conduct of the parties, including in particular *the efforts made, if any, before and during the proceedings in order to try to resolve the dispute.*

[18] http://www.justice.gov.uk/courts/procedure-rules/civil
[19] http://www.justice.gov.uk/courts/procedure-rules/civil/protocol

The pre-action protocols[19] contain standard wording on ADR, to the effect that:

> *The parties should consider whether some form of alternative dispute resolution procedure would be more suitable than litigation, and if so, endeavour to agree which form to adopt. Both the Claimant and Defendant may be required by the Court to provide evidence that alternative means of resolving their dispute were considered.*

> *The Courts take the view that litigation should be a last resort, and that claims should not be issued prematurely when a settlement is still actively being explored. Parties are warned that if this paragraph is not followed then the court must have regard to such conduct when determining costs."*

Characteristics of Mediation

Mediation is usually characterised by *without prejudice* discussions. These take place both in open (plenary) meetings with all the parties present and which the mediator will moderate, as well as in private and confidential meetings (caucuses) between individual parties, their advisers, and the mediator.

Mediations will vary in the amount of time spent in private as opposed to open sessions. There are no fixed times, structures, or patterns. During these sessions the mediator will seek to create an atmosphere where the participants focus on effective solutions rather than on past demands.

The mediator in the most commonly-used form of the process does not resemble a judge or arbitrator: the mediator neither decides who is right or wrong, nor expresses an opinion. A mediator will not give legal advice or suggest what a judge might do but instead, by using core skills, acts as a facilitator to help the participants reach a settlement which they will own.

Facilitative Mediation

Facilitative Mediation is that in which most mediators are usually trained. Training usually takes place in one intensive week and is conducted by a CMC approved training school. It does not intrinsically require the mediator to have any deep specialist knowledge of the legal context of the dispute, although many mediators will be chosen because they have professional experience. It does require the mediator to be thoroughly trained in listening and questioning skills that are often wholly alien to judges and lawyers. It is vital to understand that the mediator is not seeking to decide the case but instead to help the participants understand their own individual and common interests. Facilitative mediation is one form of a process called *Principled Negotiation*. This term was advanced by the late Professor Roger Fisher and William Ury[20] at the Harvard Negotiation Project (now the Global Negotiation Insight Initiative).

They noticed that traditional bargaining focused on defending positions rather than addressing underlying concerns. This led to a contest of wills, often resulting in a win:lose, lose:win or indeed lose:lose result.

Fisher and Ury went on to develop the technique of Principled Negotiation which centres on negotiating on merit rather than on defending or attacking positions. Principled negotiation requires the negotiator to be soft or co-operative with the people and hard on the issues. The process aims to separate the people from the problem; to focus on interests not positions; to generate a variety of options before making decisions; and to base solutions on objective criteria.

Facilitative Mediators using the Principled Negotiation model will accordingly look to distinguish between positions and interests. A good mediator will not ask a participant to give an opening position but instead to indicate what, in general terms, the participant would like to achieve from the mediation. That may lead to an agreement that both participants want a solution that is, above all, fair. Of course, getting from there to a solution is the mediator's skill but having established a common interest the process can begin.

The mediator is likely to follow this by inviting the participants to tell their stories and to listen. In doing so, the participants will be gently encouraged to put themselves in the other person's shoes and to try to see the situation as they do. The mediator will emphasise that understanding the other position is not the same as agreeing with it. Where differences exist, the mediator will encourage the participants to discuss them rationally and involve each participant in the problem-solving process - rather than trying to convince them that only one solution is right, an often ineffectual hallmark common to many client-driven litigators.

---

[20] Getting to Yes (second edition with Bruce Patton, 1997 ISBN-10: 0099248425)

From there, the mediator will look to focus on interests instead of positions. Positions are what participants actually want. Interests are why participants have decided upon the positions. Interests underline positions. To identify interests, the mediator may need to have addressed the human problems that may behind the positions: and the storytelling is indeed an important part of that process. People like or even want to be heard, especially in cases where an individual has been physically or emotionally injured or personally wronged. And one should not rule out the power of an apology in any form of business, commercial, family or other case. Humans appreciate sorry. Once a level of trust is established, the mediator can ask, usually in private and carefully avoiding any hint of opinion, probing questions that seek to reveal the active interests. Questions such as *'what is so important about this figure?'* or *'why do you need that result?'* or *'what does this mean for you personally'*? can unlock deep levels of understanding.

The mediator may also invite a participant (and their advisors) to try to imagine being in the other person's shoes – and ask why then you would or would not accept the offer. The answer can be tested against objective criteria and lead to a rapid opening of both participants' interests and the creation of possible solutions.

Appendix 4 offers The European Code of Conduct for mediators. Appendix 5 contains some practical information for legal and other advisors on the roles that they discharge: and matters to consider by which participants can prepare for Facilitative Mediation. It is not, however, the only technique that is deployed.

Evaluative Mediation

Less commonly[21] used in disputes than Facilitative Mediation, Evaluative Mediation requires the mediator to form and express an opinion on the merits and/or potential settlement terms for the dispute. This is anathema to Facilitative Mediation and needs to be considered with great care by the mediator and the participants.

It often happens that mediators, particularly lawyers or former judges who practice in specialist areas, are invited by participants (especially litigants in person) to give an evaluation or advice on some or all of the issues. Some participants want to be told *the answer* to their dispute. Some, including formerly intransigent insurers or over optimistic clients or their advisers, need the security blanket of a fresh opinion before changing their position.

---

[21] Although NB: a SCMA/CIArb meeting on 27th September 2012 reporting a perceived Trend Towards Evaluative mediation http://www.ciarb.org/events/2012/09/scma-ciarb-london-branch-joint-event/

Unless, however, the mediator has been contracted to perform an evaluative mediation, and the Mediation Agreement permits or requires such a foray, most mediators will decline to offer an evaluative opinion. Facilitative mediators hold that it is the participants who have responsibility for the problem, and who will own the solution.

If the mediator opines then the solution will not be theirs, but that of the mediator. It follows that the process is undermined by invasive opinions.

But sometimes the participants and the mediator agree in advance that the mediation should be evaluative, either from the outset or if Facilitative Mediation does not provide a solution. In that case, the Mediation Agreement must reflect this and provide for suitable measures to ensure a smooth transition to the evaluation process. So too must the means of offering the evaluation be stated: some mediators give written evaluations, others prefer to offer an oral assessment.

The means of delivery of the evaluation needs to be agreed and written into the Mediation Agreement. Sometimes, an evaluation is given to all the participants in a plenary session, somewhat akin to an arbitral award or a judge giving judgment. If this is the preferred solution, then the participants need to be aware of the implications, and particularly of the risks, of an open evaluation being given.

Most mediators prefer an assessment of the strengths and weaknesses of a case, and sometimes the likely views of a judge, to be given to each participant in private. This may avoid some of the risks of the plenary session but means that neither participant can be sure what the mediator has said to the other.

In delivering the evaluation the mediator will be at pains to emphasise the neutrality of the role and to state that any settlement proposal appears to be the best commercial solution, given the facts and opinions disclosed. The mediator will emphasise that the evaluation is non-binding and should state that the opinion given in private will be substantively identical to both participants, albeit that there may be a different emphasis in each case.

The mediator will make clear that an evaluation is made without blame or judgement. Furthermore, that where it differs from the advice previously given by the legal advisers the cause may be because the mediator has less knowledge of the case or because matters that have come to light at mediation have led to a different assessment. This can be a real problem in Evaluative Mediation because clients may find the opinion of a subject-experienced mediator to be very influential. Where the opinion differs from the advice of the instructed lawyers there may be considerable embarrassment, loss of face, or conflict. Sometimes, mindful of this dilemma, mediators will offer a range of settlements to promote further negotiation – and thereby the ownership of the solution – by the participants. This is perhaps the strongest form of Evaluative Mediation. Experienced evaluative mediators will generally not seek to justify their opinion with detailed references to facts or law. This is to avoid over-legalistic responses or challenges from participants who delve into the detail to find fault rather than to look to building a consensual solution.

Having offered an evaluation, the mediator will give participants time to consider the opinion expressed and if necessary to reassess their negotiation position. The mediator may need to devise strategies for dealing with disappointed participants to keep them engaged in solution building.

The risks of evaluative mediation must be understood. They require an informed decision by the participants and careful consideration by the mediator who should ensure that professional indemnity insurance covers such work. Competent evaluative mediators know that offering an opinion in mediation can be highly destructive to the process: once the mediator ceases to facilitate but instead assesses, the trust of and relationship with the participants may be lost. The mediator may be seen as biased, not worth dealing with, and even a hindrance to progress. Indeed, the mediation may never come to life: some mediators report that where the participants know that there may or will be an evaluation there is a reticence to open up to the mediator, to stick firmly to positions, and not to risk exposing interests. The mediator is then restricted to a very limited range of information and may have to make an evaluation based on far less information that is likely available to the court or to the participants themselves.

It follows that whilst there are some circumstances where an evaluative mediation can be effective and undertaken either from the outset or when an impasse is reached, many mediators consider that the risks outweigh the advantages. Mediators who step into the fray to offer advice, opinions, or solutions, do so at their peril.

They will be considered by many to have assumed a mantle which is hard to reconcile with the confidential neutrality of the role. They will need to be insured and prudent.

Some say their role is, to quote Sir Humphrey[22], "brave", or even "courageous".

---

[22] http://en.wikipedia.org/wiki/Yes_Minister

Mediation: a binding process?

Mediation, whether facilitative or evaluative, only produces a binding outcome if the participants agree and sign a Mediation Agreement. This document is usually provided by the mediator, as seen in Appendix 1, or could be drafted by participating legal advisers. In either case it will be contractually binding. It may be embodied in a court order where proceedings have already been commenced or where the approval of the court is required under CPR Rule 21.10[23].

Attendance at mediation is voluntary in the United Kingdom and many other jurisdictions. Mandatory schemes as pioneered in parts of Canada form no part of the domestic process. It follows that a participant is free to leave the mediation at any time if they wish, although most mediators will normally invite the participants to agree to a rule that they spend five minutes with the mediator in private before leaving, so as to find out what is wrong or to perform a final reality check. It also follows that mediations may not always lead to a settlement on the day, or in the next few days (although, as will be seen below, most do).

Mediation and confidentiality

Because of the *without prejudice* nature of mediation, if settlement is not achieved through mediation, any offers, comments, suggestions, concessions, proposals, or statements made by the participants during the course of the mediation are not binding on them and cannot be used or referred to in subsequent court proceedings. There may be rare exceptions, however, if fraud or oppression is alleged.

These questions were highlighted by the discussion of the dilemma faced by mediator Jane Andewartha in the interesting 2009 case known as *Farm Assist*[24].

Mr Justice Ramsey, though an experienced High Court judge wholly familiar with the value of mediation, set out the factors which had led him to decide that in that case the interests of justice overrode the interests of the mediator in retaining the confidentiality of what had occurred in the mediation.

The judge appears to have been particularly influenced by the fact that in support of its case DEFRA had applied illegitimate pressure or had acted in bad faith. Farm Assist Limited

---

[23] http://www.justice.gov.uk/courts/procedure-rules/civil/rules/part21
[24] Farm Assist Limited (in liquidation) v The Secretary of State for Environment, Food and Rural affairs (No.2) 2009 EWHC 1102 (TCC)

was alleging that DEFRA had refused or failed to take a structured, reasoned, bilateral, reasonable or bona fide approach to the valuation of the Farm Assist account, and that in its witness statements it was relying on what the mediator had said in private sessions, or on conversations between the mediator and others, or on what had happened in the mediation.

The judge found that whilst the mediator had said clearly that she had no recollection of the mediation, that this did not prevent her from giving evidence. He pointed out that frequently memories are jogged and recollections come to mind when documents are shown to witnesses and they have the opportunity to focus, in context, on events some years earlier.

He ended his judgment by saying that whilst the mediator had a right to rely on the confidentiality provision in the Mediation Agreement, he considered that this was a case where, as an exception, the interests of justice lay strongly in favour of evidence being given of what was said and done.

Summary

Facilitative Mediation in particular is a much used and highly valued tool for Alternative Dispute Resolution, supported in the United Kingdom and common law jurisdictions by the courts largely through contractual mechanisms. It is confidential and only exceptionally will that veil be lifted.

Mediation is highly effective, resolving seemingly intractable matters where all else has failed in a quick, quiet and cost effective way. While neither the default option nor a panacea, nor indeed a substitute for judicial precedent, for many it will be very much the future.

The mediator could see at the outset that
there would be unchecked egos to be dealt with.

Chapter 2: Why Mediate?

Introduction

According to the latest England and Wales figures for 2012, only 3.7% of issued claims proceed to trial[25]. Thus, with the vast majority of the 1.3 million cases begun settling (or being undefended or abandoned) before trial, a point raised by some advisors is why a claimant or a defendant should choose to embark on mediation at all? Why not settle at the door of the court when the pressure is at its highest, especially if there are major costs bonuses for those solicitors in doing so[26]?

The answer is that most cases, of course, do not require mediation. It is those that get stuck, for whatever reason, that do need mediation: and even those that are not stuck may benefit from the use of mediation because the participants may find a better solution in the conducive atmosphere of mediation rather than in the more fraught context of litigation.

The reasons therefore to mediate range from the benefits to the client or participant, in terms of costs, outcome, speed, reduction in hassle, and confidentiality, through to the avoidance of the negative: unforeseen penalties and risks. The courts in England and Wales have recognised this and they have available carrots and sticks, historic and future, with major changes likely throughout 2013 and 2014 to further encourage the practice of mediation.

The stick

The contemporary approach of the courts to the 'Why mediate?' question is that an unreasonable refusal of an offer of mediation will mean litigation costs. A victor who refuses to mediate may recover no costs, or there may well be other cost penalties imposed by the court.

Sir Henry Brooke, then Vice President of the Court of Appeal, and later a distinguished Chairman of the Civil Mediation Council, made this point in <u>Dunnett v Railtrack</u> [2002] EWCA Civ 302. He said:

> "Skilled mediators are now able to achieve results satisfactory to both parties in many cases that are quite beyond the power of the lawyers and courts to achieve."

[25] http://www.justice.gov.uk/statistics/courts-and-sentencing/judicial-quarterly
[26] http://www.mediates.com/drsprcnb.html

This was enlarged upon by Halsey v Milton Keynes NHS Trust [2004] EWCA Civ 576 a decision of Ward, Dyson and Laws L.JJ in the Court of Appeal. Lord Dyson has since been careful to make it clear that he values mediation and that he is neither a sceptic nor an evangelist but one who sees its usefulness in context[27]. The key question was posed at the beginning of Dyson LJ's judgement in *Halsey*:

> "*When should the court impose a costs sanction against a successful litigant on the grounds that he has refused to take part in Alternative Dispute Resolution?*"

Unsuccessful litigants who refuse mediation already faced sanctions, such as indemnity costs – see Virani v Manuel Revert [2003] EWCA Civ 1651. Indeed Dunnett v Railtrack was the first example of costs penalties being imposed on a successful litigant because of their unreasonable refusal to mediate. In *Halsey*, the party declining to mediate again escaped sanction, but the Court reviewed the circumstances in which it might do so, and confirmed its power to do so where felt appropriate. *Dunnett* remains good law, as do other cases following that decision.

Thus it still remains very important for lawyers to think carefully about advising clients whether or not to mediate a case. They may expect close questioning at case management conferences, pre-trial reviews and especially at the end of a case, as to why mediation was turned down. The answers to such questions must be informed and sophisticated.

Judges mediation training with the Judicial College (formerly the Judicial Studies Board) means that they can now be expected to understand the issues. The Civil Mediation Council has toured extensively, presenting the mechanisms for mediation and the Courts Service (now HMCTS) offers a manual on mediation to judges[28]. It follows that there is considerable awareness of the cost penalties that are available. The Courts will be further encouraged during the implementation of the Jackson Report and LASPO in 2013/14 to note the success of the Small Claims Mediation Service.

An example of an expensive day in court

The case of Rolf v De Guerin [2011] EWCA Civ 78; [2011] All ER (D) 169 (Feb) is a useful contemporary example of how a day (or more) in court with mediation unreasonably refused becomes exceptionally expensive for the winner. The Court of Appeal said:

[27] CIArb 3rd Mediation Symposium 2010
[28] http://www.judiciary.gov.uk/Resources/JCO/Documents/Guidance/civil_court_mediation_service_manual_v3_mar09.pdf

1. *This is an appeal solely about costs. It is also a sad case about lost opportunities for mediation. It demonstrates, in a particular class of dispute, how wasteful and destructive litigation can be.*

The case concerned a small building contract between a homeowner and a builder. Judge Cowell heard four days of evidence in the Central London County Court. In what was described as a very distressing dispute, on 24 June 2009 solicitors for Mrs Rolf, the homeowner, wrote to their opponents offering to attend a formal mediation with a view to discussing settlement. This was chased when no reply was received. Mediation was not accepted. The matter came before the Court of Appeal on the issue of costs. When asked why he had been unwilling to mediate, the builder, Mr Guerin, said that if he had mediated he would have had to accept *"his guilt"*; he felt he might have been unable to persuade a mediator of his case. The judge had to see that for himself at trial when he gave evidence; and in any event, *"I wanted my day in court, and I was proved correct"*.

The Court decided to allow the appeal and to exercise its discretion by making an order for no order as to costs to the winner. It had been wrong to spurn mediation and to explore settlement. Rix LJ explained this in an important way

> 41. *As for wanting his day in court, that of course is a reason why the courts have been unwilling to compel parties to mediate rather than litigate: but it does not seem to me to be an adequate response to a proper judicial concern that parties should respond reasonably to offers to mediate or settle and that their conduct in this respect can be taken into account in awarding costs.*
>
> 42. *Thus CPR 44(4) says that the court must have regard, as part of all the circumstances, to the conduct of the parties; and CPR 44(5) shows that the conduct of the parties covers a potentially wide field of enquiry. There is authority that such conduct can include the reasonableness of a response to a call for mediation, especially where the court itself (as admittedly did not occur in this case) has encouraged or recommended it.*

Rix LJ referred to <u>Burchell v. Bullard</u> [2005] EWCA Civ 358, [2005] BLR 330, [2005] 3 Costs LR 507 which concerned a dispute between a homeowner and a small builder about defects in the work. Ward LJ there said:

> [41] *…it seems to me, first, that a small building dispute is par excellence the kind of dispute which, as the recorder found, lends itself to ADR. Secondly, the merits of*

the dispute favoured mediation. The defendants behaved unreasonably in believing, if they did, that their case was so watertight that they need not engage in attempts to settle… The stated reason for refusing mediation that the matter was too complex for mediation is plain nonsense. Thirdly, the costs of ADR would have been a drop in the ocean compared with the fortune that has been spent on this litigation …

[43] … Halsey has made plain not only the high rate of a successful outcome being achieved by mediation but also its established importance as a track to a just result, running parallel to that of the court system. Both have a proper part to play in the administration of justice… The parties cannot ignore a proper request to mediate simply because it was made before the claim was issued …

Rix LJ also put the need to mediate into the contemporary context of the Jackson Review of Civil Litigation Costs: Final Report, where, at pages 298/300, the virtue of mediation is documented (see also paras 30.3.4/5 of his preliminary report).

"Encouraging ADR. Mediation is dealt with in chapter 36 below. The two principal forms of ADR are conventional negotiation and mediation. ADR has proved effective in resolving construction disputes of all sizes. In relation to small building disputes, however, it is particularly important to pursue mediation, in the event that conventional negotiation fails."

Rix LJ continued:

48. *In the present case, even the offer, often repeated, for round-table discussions was spurned. No reason was given at the time, and the reasons advanced by Mr Guerin at this appeal do not bear real examination and are unreasonable. It is possible of course that settlement discussions, or even mediation, would not have produced a solution; or would have produced one satisfactory enough to the parties to have enabled them to reach agreement but which Mr Guerin might now, with his hindsight of the judgment, have been able to say did him less than justice. Nevertheless, in my judgment, the facts of this case disclose that negotiation and/or mediation would have had reasonable prospects of success. The spurned offers to enter into settlement negotiations or mediation were unreasonable and ought to bear materially on the outcome of the courts discretion, particularly in this class of case.*

49. *In these circumstances, I consider that an order for no order as to costs does substantial justice between the parties. Indeed, I would not have been averse to an order somewhat, but not by very much, in favour of Mrs Rolf, if it were not for the fact that, on appeal, this court should recognise that, even though it may, as here, be fully entitled to exercise its discretion afresh, it should recognise the limitations under which it suffers as not being the court of trial; and if it were not also for the fact that, as Mr Pringle himself realistically accepts, an order in favour of Mrs Rolf would be unlikely to produce real results.*

The case of <u>Rolf v De Guerin</u> is referred to in the model mediation offer letter in Appendix 1 to this book. It is likely to form the basis for future offers over the next few years.

Court-ordered mediation

In *Halsey*, the court said that to fail to mediate after recommendation by the Court to do so could well, of itself, justify a costs sanction against a successful party. Master Ungley[29] designed an order which does much the same thing.

The Ungley order reads:

> *The parties shall by [date] consider whether the case is capable of resolution by mediation. If any party considers that the case is unsuitable for resolution by mediation, that party shall be prepared to justify that decision at the conclusion of the trial, should the judge consider that such means of resolution were appropriate, when he is considering the appropriate costs order to make.*

> *The party considering the case unsuitable for mediation shall, not less than 28 days before the commencement of the trial, file with the court a witness statement without prejudice save as to costs, giving reasons upon which they rely for saying that the case was unsuitable.*

A party seeking to maximise costs recovery should, after a claim is issued, therefore seek a court order recommending mediation. Any party ignoring this may well face costs sanctions.

---

[29] A Master is a procedural judge of the High Court in England and Wales.

When can an offer to mediate be refused?

Halsey essentially looks at cases where there is no Court Order to mediate. It makes it clear that although to deprive a successful party of costs is an exception to the CPR 44.3(2) that costs follow the event, the power still exists to do so on the basis of unreasonable conduct.

Indeed, variations on traditional costs orders because of unreasonable litigation conduct, lack of proportionality or failure to win on certain issues – and occupying court time doing so, have become commonplace since the CPR.

The Court in *Halsey* identified six factors which might be considered as justifying refusal to mediate when determining costs issues:

> (1) **The nature of the dispute,** as to which the Court warned that "*most cases are not, by their very nature, unsuitable for mediation.*"

> (2) **The merits of the case,** by which a party which reasonably believes it has an overwhelming case might make refusal of mediation reasonable. Where a case is border-line, refusal is much riskier.

> (3) **Other settlement methods have been attempted,** though again the Court noted that "*mediation often succeeds where other settlement attempts have failed*", and it regards this reason as part of whether mediation has reasonable prospects of success.

> (4) **Costs of mediation would be disproportionately high** which may sometimes be a proper consideration late in a modest claim, but the cost benefit is usually incontestable before, or in the early to mid-stages of litigation.

> (5) **Delay** to a trial date: this is rare, and successful mediations have been arranged many times in the last weeks, days, or even hours before a trial.

> (6) **Whether mediation had a reasonable prospect of success:** the burden of proof lies with the unsuccessful party who proposed mediation, and not with the successful party who refused. This factor is actually rather played down by the Court in *Halsey*, since it may be the attitude of a party which means that mediation has no reasonable prospect of success.

The burden is not regarded by the Court as being unduly onerous: the unsuccessful litigant must show that there was a reasonable prospect that the mediation would have succeeded. What amounts to 'success' in mediation remains open to debate.

Other reasons for refusal that might be regarded as reasonable include cases where injunctive relief is required (and there is no offer of an undertaking being agreed), where a court is required as a matter of law (although a joint proposed consent order can often be a sensible outcome) and where a decision is required on a new matter of law. Sometimes allegations of criminal conduct, or cases where there is suspected money-laundering, will be proper causes for mediation to be rejected.

These are not, however, likely to be the norm. Most cases, as the judges recognise in all the examples set out above, are suitable for mediation rather than litigation. There are, in addition to the costs imperatives that follow judicial authority, strong human and tactical reasons for using mediation.

The Carrot

The Clinical Disputes Forum[30] (reviewing mediation in clinical negligence cases in the United Kingdom) suggests that for claimants involved in an often extremely personal dispute, mediation offers a guaranteed opportunity to be involved in the negotiation process and to discuss the issues face to face with the other people involved. Mediation enables the claimant (or a bereaved family) a chance to meet with – and be heard by – the defendant team who will, it is generally expected, come with authority to settle the claim, if they are or can be persuaded that it is right to do so.

At mediation, claimants can express not only how they feel about what happened, but also their wishes for the future in an often emotional, disjointed, and personal manner, using non-technical language. They are not constrained by the formal requirements of a witness statement or court rules. They can unload the angst or anger they may have been feeling and this cathartic process, although sometimes self-defeating, can lead to a greater willingness to settle a claim on more realistic terms.

Against a climate where there is less willingness on the part of courts and the government to encourage trials, mediation provides the opportunity for the aggrieved person to *have their day in court* in a manner which was often reserved for the opening 30 minutes of

[30] http://www.clinical-disputes-forum.org.uk/project.asp?projectid=5

evidence in chief in pre-Civil Procedure Rules days. The Forum recognised that defendants too are able to talk directly to the claimant, explaining on a purely without prejudice basis, sometimes for the first time, what happened, how things have changed and any appropriate regret, without necessarily having to concede liability or offer compensation. For clinicians, mediation can offer a satisfying closure to what is often the considerable burden of facing an accusation of professional negligence. All of this takes place in an entirely safe environment: informal, private and off the record.

It is widely recognised that what is valid in the clinical negligence context is equally true in business, property, commercial, family, employment, and insurance matters: indeed any sector where there is a need to separate the people from the problem and to consider motive, interests, and other human factors in anything other than a purely mechanical manner. Classically, other reasons to mediate include:

(a) when the participants have conflicting views of the facts or law.

(b) when a participant needs to express strong emotions.

(c) when a participant craves the opportunity to be heard directly by the opposing participant.

(d) When clients or their lawyers can no longer effectively communicate with each other without the assistance of a skilful mediator.

(e) When the participants are not skilful negotiators and need the process structure and negotiation expertise provided by a mediator.

(f) When a conflict exists between a participant and his or her lawyer.

This last reason is often underestimated by defendants who may be surprised at the number of claimants who, in the views of their lawyers, have unreasonable expectations are seeking a manner other than trial to obtain an external reality check and settlement.

---

[31] Roger Fisher & Daniel Shapiro, Beyond Reason: Using Emotions As You Negotiate (2005)

In respect of strong emotional cases, some mediators baulk at the cases suitability for mediation. Many others, however, would agree with the late Professor Roger Fisher, the founder of the Harvard International Negotiation Program Daniel Shapiro,[31] in his astute analysis of emotional cases. He found that it is in highly emotional claimant side cases where mediation can be most effective. They may there deploy what Jeff Kichaven[32] describes as the magical paradox to assist a claimant who is paralysed by emotions or who has deep fears to unlock. He suggests the mediator asks the participant a question such as:

> I bet you feel that nobody knows what this situation has done to you, how it has broken you up inside, and made it difficult for you to believe that you will ever be able to have a normal life again Is that so?

Here, reflective listening is likely to promote valuable feedback. Empathetic listening, without implying agreement or loss of neutrality, is seen as important tools in cases which can be especially difficult to resolve. These skills are fundamental parts of contemporary mediator training, although of course the words, language, and tone will vary with the participants and the mediator.

At the tactical level

At the tactical level, and beyond the obvious opportunity to settle the case, mediation offers a number of clear opportunities which are unlikely to be available except in so short a time, or at one opportunity. These include:

(a) **Common ground:** the chance for the participants to establish negotiations based on common information and to avoid misunderstandings, or poor assessments of what the other case may be.

(b) **Reality testing:** mediation may be the first time that a participant, often the claimant, has the opportunity to, or is forced to, consider the claim against objective criteria clearly expressed. A skilled mediator will, without expressing any opinion, cause the participant to explain why a particular position is held.

The use of the word *why?* is such a powerful tool by a neutral: *I am going to win* or *I want ten grand* tested by that short question, repeated as the answers unfold, can

---

[32] of IMRI, writing for www.mediate.com

lead to a process in which the participant is confronted with the possibly that a judge may make adverse findings, with the effect on damages and costs (as well as the intangible psychological consequences) that such an outcome may have.

Most mediators will cite many cases as examples where reluctant defendants have found to their surprise that claimants who have been intractable can, at mediation, come to settle their claim at a reasonable level. Usually, reality testing, combined with the added value items of apologies and other assurances, are the reasons for such changes of heart.

(c) **Information gathering:** whilst no reference can be made to matters divulged or discussed for the first time at mediation in a later trial, there is no embargo on a participant acting upon intelligence gained at mediation. Increasingly, sophisticated participants, mainly defendants, and their advisors will enter mediation to learn about the claimant and use the information for the tactical management of the claim if it does not settle. There is nothing improper in these 'fishing trips' and participants must consider what is or is not discussed or disclosed and bear these risks in mind.

(d) **Clarifying, making, or refining offers:** this may appear a trite reason for attending mediation but for astute participants the opportunity to make an offer at mediation is far better than making such an offer in correspondence. This is for two reasons:

1. The offeror has a final chance to size-up the other participant and make adjustments to the offer he or she would make in the light of what is seen and heard; sometimes, spectacular savings can be achieved, especially if the claimant in opening makes a substantial concession or suggests that an apology or some other intangible matter is what is primarily sought.

2. The offeror has the immediate opportunity to gauge the impact of the offer on the other participant, especially if the offer is delivered across the table in the plenary session; by making a low offer, which may be ignored in correspondence, the offeror can assess by the reactions what may be sufficient to tip the balance in circumstances where there are a range of risks.

(e) **Exploring extra-judicial opportunities:** as discussed above, mediation provides to participants an opportunity to consider a range of solutions not open to a court. These may include items which add value at little or no cost to the paying party and yet make a clear difference to the overall solution to the claimant.

These include apologies, treatment, policy reviews, retraining, research, contribution to knowledge databases, staff redeployment, and other intangibles.

(f) **Planning CPR Part 36[33] offers and payments:** mediation offers, even in cases where no settlement is achieved, the chance for both participants to re-assess or to plan CPR Part 36 offers or payments based on intelligence gained. Very often participants are concerned to obtain maximum protection with minimum risk and the ability to pitch a CPR Part 36 offer just below the threshold which a participant will not accept may be tactically astute in some cases.

Although it is right to recognise that some participants therefore use mediation to explore the limits of the other side's case and then plot an offer just outside what they might consider acceptable once the process is over. Of course, participants may be alive to this tactical exploration and have their own responses but it is nevertheless a potentially challenging approach if the claim will not settle on other terms.

In all of this, however, it constantly surprises mediators and indeed participants that the intention to use a mediation tactically for *fishing trips* or some other purpose with little intention to settle is subjugated to wider strategic options. Very few mediations, conducted through interest–based facilitation fail against pure stonewalling tactics.

Summary

Overall, there are very few real reasons not to mediate where conventional court negotiation is not progressing. These reasons will be diminished further in England and Wales over the next few years following the civil justice reforms and cases such as <u>Rolf v De Guerin</u>. The same applies in many other jurisdictions around the world.

So, it is on the positive reason to mediate that we should focus. The range of extra-judicial outcomes, the confidentiality, speed, and savings in costs and management time, the saving or recovering of relationships, the keeping of control with the participants (as opposed to

---

[33] CPR Part 36 is the formal process of making an offer in litigation in England or Wales which if rejected and not beaten will result in cost sanctions.

handing it to a judge or an arbitrator) are all particularly strongly acclaimed features of mediation.

It is also right to recognise that when engaged in litigation, lawyers can be exceptionally destructive while acting for their clients: but when engaged in mediation it is remarkable how they can act collaboratively to create sensible, sensitive and lasting solutions. It is a role that no lawyer should shirk or fail to enjoy.

As the Second Edition went to print the English Court of Appeal handed down its seminal judgment in the case of <u>PGF II SA v OMFS Company 1 Limited</u> [20013] EWCA Civ 1288. The appeal raised, for the first time as a matter of principle, the following question: what should be the response of the court to a party which, when invited by its opponent to take part in a process of mediation, simply declines to respond to the invitation in any way?

The Court of Appeal has now, in *PGF II SA*, gone considerably further than Halsey mentioned above: it upheld the depriving of a successful party of more than £500,000 in costs because of its conduct in refusing to explore, or to engage in, mediation. As Briggs LJ (giving the unanimous judgment of the Court) said, in the final paragraph:

"...this case sends out an important message to civil litigants, requiring them to engage with a serious invitation to participate in ADR, even if they have reasons which might justify a refusal, or the undertaking of some other form of ADR, or ADR at some other time in the litigation. To allow the present appeal would, as it seems to me, blunt that message. The court's task in encouraging the more proportionate conduct of civil litigation is so important in current economic circumstances that it is appropriate to emphasise that message by a sanction which, even if a little more vigorous than I would have preferred, nonetheless operates pour encourager les autres."

In the authors' opinion, it represents a sea change – and should be cited with relish by proponents of mediation, and rightly feared by those who prefer the traditional, and expensive route, of maximising costs before settling at the door of the court. It was an important day for common law civil justice.

*"The Mediation Time Warp: They start out
as adults...Regress to children screaming 'mine'...
Then grow up again and compromise...hopefully."*

Chapter 3: When to Mediate?
And When Not to Mediate

For mediation to be successful, some authors say hold that all the participants in a dispute need to have sufficient information available to them, before they start, to form a view as to whether settlement is appropriate. But many lawyers and advisors well know that clients are often prepared to pay a significant premium for early resolution even when the professionals consider it premature, because of the hidden costs of delay, hassle, exposure, distraction, effect on business, and morale or relationship damage.

The timing of a mediation

Mediation can be considered at any stage before or during the litigation process. There are many reasons and advantages for it being at a very early stage in simpler cases, or slightly later in more document-based disputes. It is rarely too early or too late, but, in particular, once lawyers are involved, consideration should be given to:

(1) **In minor cases,** as early as there is sufficient evidence to satisfy the paying party of the probity of the case and the claimant's advisors that there is not a longer-term claim waiting in the wings.

(2) **Following completion of the Pre-Action Protocol**[34] **process:** some evidence will usually have been obtained at this stage and depending on how far the case is distant there may be a reasonable feel for losses and expenses.

(3) **Once the claim has been issued,** and the Court has allocated the matter, then there may well be an invitation from the court to mediate under the court scheme or to consider mediation. Such an invitation commonly requires a response to the District Judge and may, if declined, require an explanation at a subsequent Case Management Conference: a party declining to mediate would do well to have in mind the reasons for a party reasonably to refuse mediation as set out in Halsey v Milton Keynes NHS Trust (see Section 3, above).

(4) **Whenever settlement negotiations have broken down:** this may seem trite but for the reasons set out in Chapter 2, the other legal advisor may welcome a mediation proposal as a means of providing the necessary reality test for their client.

---

[34] Or other pre-issue or summons stages – these vary in different jurisdictions but in the England and Wales jurisdiction are set out at: http://www.justice.gov.uk/courts/procedure-rules/civil/protocol

(5) **Before the final build up to trial,** in an attempt to avoid an expensive or protracted hearing. It is rarely the case in significant disputes exceeding £100,000 that the cost of mediation will be more than 20% of the cost of a trial with two or more experts involved. Frequently, in a case with two experts lasting three days, costs between Pre-Trial Review and the end of the trial will (on both sides) exceed £50,000, excluding the loss of witness time.

In contrast, £2,500 will fund a skilled mediator for six hours work. No experts will be required. It follows that even if only half of mediations settled at this late stage there would be substantial costs and stress savings.

In every case, a proper review of the underlying interests and needs should be conducted by both parties in assessing whether the simple, all or nothing approach of proceeding to trial is in the end the most effective. This will include analysis of the costs and benefits of mediation compared with those of trial.

(6) **When an offer to mediate is received** and it would not be considered by a costs judge to be reasonable to refuse to mediate. In this respect, see the discussion in Chapter 2 surrounding *Halsey* and the model mediation offer letter in Appendix 1.

Overall, there are numerous opportunities to mediate. There are few occasions when it will be wrong to do so.

Lawyers and advisors are frequently surprised that their clients prefer a good enough solution achieved at mediation, with the values of certainty, time-saving, and the absence of risk, to a rights-based judgment achieved months or years later at trial. Professionals will therefore wish to have a clear understanding of the cost-benefits of mediation and the potential strategic and tactical advantages of an pre-trial offer.

They threw a surprise mediation for Ted.

Chapter 4: Who Should Mediate?

There are at least 2,000 people practising as mediators, in the civil, commercial, employment, and workplace areas of work across the United Kingdom – or at least holding themselves out as willing to take instructions to mediate. Perhaps 200 in all fields are full-time, many are part-timers alongside a professional role, and some are occasional individual practitioners.

There are many more family, special education and disability needs and community mediators who specialise in the narrower, but challenging fields of difficulties in relationships or needs. Many work unpaid but because mediation is not a regulated profession it is impossible to be sure precisely how many mediators are practicing across the country.

Many of the cohorts of mediators are excellent: both objectively and in the feedback they receive from participants. Some are newly-trained, some are still novices even after a few years and of course a few are somewhat less than impressive. There are very few complaints about mediators received by the Civil Mediation Council: but when they are, they tend to focus on perceptions of bias, poor administration, or a belief that inadequate interest was shown in the process.

Presently in the United Kingdom there is no limitation on who can use the title mediator. There are those who profess to be mediators who have done no formal training. There are mediators who have undertaken different kinds of training for different kinds of dispute. Some have trained for a couple of hours, some have trained for many years. It is essential therefore to make inquiries of any potential mediator before agreeing to engage them.

Mediators come in all shapes and sizes. Some are lawyers, many (including some of the best) are not. Some specialise in certain dispute areas, many are generalists undertaking any type of dispute. There are full time mediators who mediate weekly, and part-time mediators who mediate a few times a year.

There are very young mediators, some still in tertiary education, and others who train as mediators when they retire from their original profession. All will bring different qualities and skills to mediation.

How do mediators train?

The Civil Mediation Council (CMC) recognises the major training organisations[35] who provide civil and commercial mediation training. The recognised training organisations

[35] See Appendix 7

provide a minimum of 40 hours face-to-face mediation training, which is independently assessed. Qualified mediators should have a certificate of successful completion of training. The criteria are reviewed regularly and were established after academically-moderated debate over an extended period of time[36].

Lists of individual mediators

The CMC maintains a list of its individual mediator members at www.civilmediation.org. This comprises individuals who have paid an annual fee[37] and submitted their details, which are carefully scrutinised by the registrar. There is no quality assessment.

The National Mediator Database (NMD), www.nationalmediatordatabase.com maintains a list of mediators who have completed recognised civil and commercial mediation training. Mediators must lodge their training certificate before appearing on the database as well as evidence of Continuous Professional Development (CPD) and insurance. Listing on the NMD is free although if a mediator is appointed through the NMD the mediator will pay a percentage of the fee to the NMD for administration.

The Bar Council maintains a list of barrister mediators which lists barristers who are mediators by experience and by fields of interest. There is no fee for listing. The Mediation Directory can be found at www.barcouncil.org.uk/about-the-bar/find-a-barrister/mediation-directory.

There are numerous individual or independent mediators who are not listed on these databases, or similar ones operated by a variety of bodies, who still have significant practises. *Google* or other search engine entries disclose these in abundance: and there are listed later in this chapter criteria which users may wish to apply in selecting mediators from databases, panels, the internet or other sources of knowledge.

Who chooses the mediator?

The participants in the mediation agree who the mediator will be. Usually, but not always, the party suggesting mediation will nominate several mediators for the other participant to consider. These may be mediators they have used before, mediators that have been recommended to them, or names they have found on the resources mentioned here.

---

[36] See Appendix 2

[37] CMC Individual Membership in 2012 was £75 per annum

Mediators on panels

An alternative for those seeking mediation is to go to a mediation provider. This is an organisation such as CEDR, ADR Group, National Mediation, Core Solutions, National Mediation, or Trust Mediation (and at least 75 more that are readily known to be of repute in the United Kingdom), that keeps a list of mediators on their panel. The CMC offers to accredit Mediation Providers who meet certain minimum but essential criteria: see www. civilmediation.org and Appendix 2 below.

A Mediation Provider may charge an administration fee for one of their panel mediators to be engaged. For this they can be expected to manage the mediation, to provide information and billing, to arrange matters such as a venue (albeit that a fee may be charged for the venue) and to provide CVs and other information. They are generally very knowledgeable about their mediators and can provide useful background, guidance, and conflict checks.

Some providers require mediators on their panels to be exclusive to their organisation: that though is generally more common in the United States. It is not often found in the United Kingdom and mediators will often welcome direct approaches from potential users.

In the workplace arena, the CMC maintains a list of registered workplace mediators at www.cmcregistered.org, which is a scrutinised list of workplace providers, more details of which are at Appendix 7. Most workplace providers also offer employment mediation and are registered to this website.

These organisations may have as few as two or three mediators but the mediators can often be very skilled and experienced.

Family and community panels are equally abundant: the College of Mediators and the Family Mediation Council have significant lists and set standards and criteria for membership. Community mediation groups are best searched for on Google.

How to select a mediator

If a participant has been provided with a list of nominated mediators to consider, or has compiled a short-list, it is important to ensure that due diligence is undertaken before agreeing to a particular mediator being instructed. Participants should not be afraid to telephone each mediator on the short-list to ask them to describe their approach, their style, and their manner.

Most mediators are very happy to enter a beauty contest and provided participants do not attempt to discuss the case itself, will answer all approach and administrative questions. If they will not, thought should be given as to whether the individual will be the best mediator on the day.

Questions to consider include:

(1) **Lawyer or non-lawyer:** mediations do not necessarily need to have a mediator who has been legally trained. Some of the very best mediators have never been to law school; in fact a whole organisation now exists for them, the Non-Lawyer Mediation Group, www.nlmg.com.

It is important for participants to remember that a mediator is not engaged to determine the issues or hand down a decision. The mediator's role is almost always restricted to facilitating a resolution through reflective listening and fostering principled negotiation against a reality-checking process. Trust, tact, rapport, diplomacy, and patience, combined with listening skills and an understanding and belief in the process may outweigh any knowledge of the Court rules set out in *The White Book*[38]. Mediators who combine these seminal qualities with relevant legal awareness may offer the best of both worlds for some participants.

(2) **Specialist or generalist:** an always open question is whether a mediator needs to be a specialist in the field at the heart of the dispute. The answer depends on the character and experience of the mediator and the characters and needs of the participants. The more skilled and experienced in the surprising range of issues that emerge in mediation the practitioner is, the less important professional specialism appears to become.

(3) **Trust and rapport:** It is important when selecting a mediator to find a person with whom the participants feel able to work[39]. Mediators have different styles and personalities and not all will suit every participant. As discussed above, mediators are generally open to informal discussions as to their style and approach and this can greatly assist the early development of confidence.

[38] *The White Book* is Sweet and Maxwell's guide to Civil Procedure
[39] See eg: ASAUK's guidance at http://www.asauk.org.uk/fileLibrary/pdf/Findingandchoosing.pdf

(4) **Novice or veteran:** some participants in a mediation only want the most experienced, and therefore often the most expensive, mediators. Others simply want the opportunity to engage a neutral who has the skills needed to facilitate a constructed conversation. In the same way that many trainee solicitors and pupil barristers are wholly competent, newly qualified mediators can often be (with good training) very effective indeed.

(5) **The question of conflict:** it is fundamental that a mediator must be neutral but this does not mean that a mediator cannot know a participant or their representatives, company, or products. The question is whether the mediator really is conflicted, either by perception or in some other substantive manner.

In the workplace, or in specialist fields of law such a personal injury, the mediator is often known to the participants professionally. Because the mediator does not decide anything it is seldom a significant issue. If it is, the mediator either refuses to accept the instruction, or if they have accepted it when the conflict emerges, the mediator steps down.

Questions to ask of a prospective mediator

Typically, participants will want a CV before speaking to the potential mediator. All mediators and Mediation Providers should have these available if they are not displayed on their websites. These will guide potential users to the knowledge of where and when the mediator trained, how many mediations the mediator has done, and their general background and inclinations.

It is permissible to ask the mediator for their success rate, if by success it is meant whether there have been resolutions on the day or shortly thereafter. Most mediators do not advertise this because there is a consensus that mediators should have no pressure upon them to maintain or improve success by falling into a temptation to pressure participants to settle for their own reasons. It is also the case that very often the mediator has little control over the prospects of success. Those who work in trenchant family disputes, or look to assist in neighbourhood issues, or in matters concerning particularly avarice driven accident victims, may have an apparently lower success rate; this does not reflect at all on their abilities.

There are, however, mediators with hundreds of cases to their name, who use absolutely no pressure and only use the best facilitation techniques, who have a better than 90% success rate across all manner of cases. It cannot always be through luck.

Fees and hidden costs

These are covered in more detail in Chapter 5 but it is important that potential users ensure that they are certain what fees are being charged, whether there is an additional fee for any room hire and refreshments, whether the mediator will also charge for reading the papers beforehand and what happens if the mediation runs later than planned.

Overtime, travel, and miscellaneous expenses should all be covered in the fee quote but sometimes are unread and become an unwelcome issue later. It is worthwhile establishing whether the mediator is to be paid in advance or on account.

In Summary

Those wishing to engage a mediator may wish to:

(a) Choose a mediator from a CMC Accredited or Registered Mediation Provider.

(b) Choose a mediator who is listed as an individual member of the CMC or other reputable body.

(c) Choose a mediator who works under the European Code of Conduct.[40]

(d) Consider whether a mediator with a legal background is needed.

(e) Obtain CVs and call candidate mediators to get a feel for personality, approach, and success rate.

(f) Use novice mediators who have specialisms but little mediation experience.

[40] See Appendix 4

(g) Not be concerned as to specialisation if the mediator is very experienced.

(h) Check what is included in the fee and get the quote in writing; and

(i) Relax: statistics show that they have at least a 90% chance of a settlement being reached in most areas of dispute where mediation is used.

*Mediation was always a challenge when the case
was between the firms of Mongoose, Mongoose &
Mongoose and Cobra, Cobra & Cobra.*

Chapter 5: How Much is Mediation?

Introduction

This Chapter deals with the fees charged by mediators in different types of cases in the United Kingdom. It also considers the additional costs and charges associated with mediation generally. There is, however, an open and competitive market place with no fixed fee structure or limit on fees. This chapter should be taken as a guide and potential users of mediation, or mediators considering what charges to make, should ensure that there is a transparency and awareness before and when the Mediation Agreement[41] (the contract that governs the mediation) is signed.

It is also worth considering that whilst mediators may have widely differing levels of experience in mediation, few have trained and worked exclusively as a mediator throughout their career. It follows that the potential users of a mediator are engaging them not simply for their mediation experience: there may be very substantial relevant training or background professional knowledge contributing to the fees charged. Novice mediators may well charge fees no different to those with very high numbers of mediations to their name if they can justify the remuneration.

Potential users of mediation may find that the quality of the mediation is not price dependent. Many fine mediators work for free for *pro bono* charities. Publically minded Community Mediators may charge as little as 10% or 20% of what other mediators may charge for a commercial or financial mediation. Equally, some exceptional mediators charge more than £10,000 per day to help resolve disputes in which their fee is of no consequence given the sums at stake. According to CEDR's 2012 fifth biannual audit of civil and commercial mediators,[42] the average fees of the less experienced mediator group for a one-day mediation have increased from around £1,390 in 2010 to £1,517, an increase of 9.1% over a two year period. The average fees for more experienced mediators rose 24% from £3,450 in 2010 to £4,279 in 2012.

Fixed-fee and hourly rate mediation

There is, properly, no consistency as between providers, or individual mediators as charge by fixed fee or by hourly rate. Some organisations charge fixed fees, inclusive of preparation, reasonable travel, the mediation, and a set number of hours. Sometimes this varies with the value of the dispute: but not always. It is also important to check if the fees quoted are per party, or per mediation.

[41] See Chapter 1
[42] www.cedr.com/news/7391

Thus, (as unendorsed examples of fixed fees, as of 1st November 2012):

- **Trust Mediation** (www.trustmediation.org.uk) working nationally in personal injury and clinical negligence disputes publishes its charges as follows:

    4 hour mediation – the mediator is paid £1,350 plus VAT.

    8 hour mediation – the mediator is paid £2,500 plus VAT.

    It charges £300 more to administer the process to cover its costs. Preparation, reading, mediators travel, and the mediation of up to four or eight hours are included in the fee. The venue for the mediation, and any cost for the venue and refreshments, is the responsibility of the parties.

- **Clerksroom** (www.clerksroom.com) which is reportedly the busiest supplier of mediation services taking all sectors and sizes of dispute into account, publishes its fixed fee scheme as follows:

    £500 *per party* (£1,000 in all for two parties) plus VAT for a full day for cases up to £50,000 in value with administration, preparation and travel included. The cost of the venue is not included.

    £1,250 *per party* (£2,500 in all for two parties) plus VAT for cases £50,000 to £250,000 in value, including one of its venues, administration, preparation and travel.

    £1,750 *per party* (£3,500 in all for two parties) plus VAT for high value cases including one of its venues, administration, preparation, travel and a mediator with at least 50 mediations on their CV.

- **National Mediation** (www.nationalmediation.com) publishes a fixed fee based on the value of dispute that varies from:

£1,500 plus VAT all inclusive (except venue) for disputes valued under £50,000;

£2,500 plus VAT all inclusive (except venue) for disputes of over £50,000 and less than £500,000;

£3,500 plus VAT all inclusive (except venue) for disputes of over £500,000.

Long established ADR Group (www.adr-group.co.uk) offer both fixed per party fees and negotiable hourly rates[43]. Many other civil and commercial providers are relatively discreet as to fees. On their websites, by way of examples only, as at 1st November 2012:

- **CEDR-solve** (www.cedr.com/solve/fees/) says:

  "Fees – Please call or email if you require guidance on fees".

- **The Academy of Experts** (www.academyofexperts.org) says:

  "Cost of mediation – This depends mainly on the time estimate and amount involved. A simple half day case might cost as little as £500 (plus VAT) for each side, plus the cost of the room, and the mediator's travel expenses."

- **The Chartered Institute of Arbitrators** (www.ciarb.org) charges £600 to organise the mediation and the parties undertake to pay the mediators "reasonable fees" before the mediation.

- **The Royal Institute of Chartered Surveyors** (www.rics.org) offers a per party fixed fee guideline scheme in disputes up to £50,000 and thereafter the fees will "need to need to be agreed with RICS".

In terms of hourly rates, typical charges are between £100+VAT per hour to £500+VAT per hour, or more. The hourly rate may be applied to travel, waiting, and the mediation day: terms and conditions need to be carefully checked. There may be additional costs of overnight accommodation and travel expenses. There are, of course, more than 75

[43] http://www.adrgroup.co.uk/images/library/files/commercial/Fee_Guide.pdf

other civil and commercial providers, at least fifty workplace providers, and hundreds of individual mediators whose fees can be sought using a search engine. They vary with region, experience, and type of dispute.

A search conducted on 31st December 2012 suggested that the lowest fee offered for a mediation involving civil or commercial issues was £500+VAT all inclusive for a case worth less than £25,000 in Leeds and £750+VAT all inclusive, except for venue, where the sum involved was less than £50,000 in Manchester. In other words where there were two paying parties, they would pay £250+VAT or £375+VAT each should they choose that mediator.

The question of quality against fees provokes considerable debate amongst mediators: and there emerges some resentment amongst full-time mediators at the influx of part-time mediators who can afford to charge lower fees may affect their livelihood. This tension, which exists in many occupations, is not likely to be resolved, or regulated, by the CMC or by the government which appears keen to leave such matters to the market-place.

So too are the fees levied by providers sometimes an issue: some (as illustrated above) charge a separate administration fee for additional services.

Others simply collect a percentage of the mediator's fee – this varies from 10% at Clerksroom to 60% at some international organisations now working in London.

Extras

It will be seen the range of options available mean that care should be taken by those engaging a mediator to ensure the instructions and charges are clear and explained before the mediation. In particular, venue costs, travel expenses and overnight accommodation can be significant and should not be forgotten.

After conventional negotiation techniques failed,
they moved to the mediator's pool for a chicken fight.

Chapter 6: Where to Mediate?
Location, location, location!

There has been considerable academic debate[44] about mediation location – whether some locations are better than others for mediation and what if anything can be done to create a climate for settlement.

Mediation can take place anywhere. Mediators will recount experiences of convening mediations in a sodden field, on a beach, on a building site, onboard a ship, in a departure lounge, and on an island in the Andaman Sea. There will be plenty of more bizarre examples. There are no rules or rigid requirements.

Usually, however, mediations require some degree of privacy, with places where the participants can discuss matters confidentially with the mediator when the need arises. As a rule they take place on neutral ground but there is no inherent objection to any location. Thus, options include using one of the participants' solicitor's offices; a hotel; a private home; or a village hall – the list goes on.

Distractions may exist, however, and the greater benefit may be derived from a bespoke mediation centre, or court facilities, if these are convenient. Many law firms and barristers chambers also offer mediation rooms at a modest fee or on a *quid pro quo* arrangement.

If people do not feel safe in the mediation process, they will be unlikely to participate effectively. Madonik states[45] that feelings about safety and control begin before the mediation, and end when the parties arrive safely at home afterwards. Accordingly, she recommends that mediators encourage those organising the venue to:

- Provide maps and directions to the location.

- Choose a site accessible by private and public transportation.

- Choose a site that people will perceive as safe after dark.

- Tell participants in advance if parking is limited and provide, if possible, free parking passes.

- Advise participants of the location of bathrooms, phones, and fire exits.

[44] For example: Paula Young, 2007 - http://www.mediate.com/articles/young19.cfm

[45] I Hear What You Say, But What are You Telling Me? Strategic Use of Nonverbal Communication in Mediation (Jossey-Bass Pub. 2001).

- Survey participants in advance to learn of any special needs, such as:

  Handicap access

  Child care needs

  Translators, or

  Special dietary requirements.

There was some debate in the CMC as to whether mediators would have to fund the special needs of any of the participants. Careful consideration of the relevant legislation, including the Equality Act 2010, means that it is the responsibility of those contracting with the mediator to provide, for example, a signer or a translator but this does not mean that mediators should not check for the need for, or the reality of, such provision.

Basic requirements

Early questions to inform the choice of venue will have to bear in mind disabled access and the numbers of people attending the mediation. It is worth considering that anyone may attend as long as the participants consent. There will certainly be the participants, perhaps their immediate family, perhaps their legal team, including any trainees or pupils, perhaps other advisers, and of course the mediator and any mediation observers. It follows that one room will need to be large enough to accommodate everyone who will sit in the open/ plenary session. There should be sufficient chairs for this purpose.

Each set of participants will need a room where they can retreat to work in private. It is not acceptable to expect participants to work in a common area such as a reception area or thoroughfare. Again the rooms need to be suitable for the number of occupants.

Often, if participants have legal advisors, a room will be set aside for the mediator. It is in fact a rarity that a mediator will need the luxury of such a room since the mediator will generally be working with one participant or another. The mediator can usually make do with the plenary/main meeting room if space is at a premium.

Breakout space

There may be occasions when the mediator is asked to meet one or more legal teams without their respective clients, or vice versa. If the participants consent to this, then those leaving the room will need somewhere to convene and may not wish to convene together. Reception areas or breakout space may be required.

Distance between rooms

The rooms should be reasonably proximate, preferably on the same floor of a building, as the mediator will need to move between the participant's rooms. Valuable mediation time may be lost if participants are accommodated on different floors, or in different buildings, although in some rare cases there may be good reasons for this to be so.

The rooms should ideally not be adjacent to one another to ensure that there is sufficient sound proofing to prevent confidential information from being inadvertently disclosed. Opposite sides of a corridor, or a room in between participant's rooms works well. It is not acceptable to expect participants to work in rooms with non-soundproof partitions.

Open windows

In modern, sealed, air-conditioned premises, open windows are unlikely to be an issue: but in many places, it is important to consider how far sound can travel. In summer or in warm weather, it can be tempting to open windows, whilst inadvertently throwing away confidentiality.

Interruptions

Rooms should be clearly marked as occupied, and other occupants in the vicinity of the mediation rooms should be briefed to ensure that there are no unnecessary interruptions.

Facilities

The participants should have access to a telephone and Internet access in their mediation rooms as they may need to make or receive calls or access resources.

It is trite but true to observe that people work better when they are comfortable and refreshed. Tea, coffee and water should be readily available, with lunch provided if working over the lunch period. Access and egress, and catering out of hours may need to be considered if working beyond standard office times.

Recording equipment

Participants should check that any recording equipment in the rooms is disabled. Video conferencing has, in more than one location, been found to have been recording enabled inadvertently or inappropriately.

Is the venue conducive to resolution?

Sometimes participants agree to mediate in an opponent's office, only to find that the hosts are placed in the relatively palatial board room, whilst the visitors are asked to work in a small room under the stairs which has no windows or air conditioning. Such imbalances may be intended to send signals, but mediators will wish to consider whether the hosts intending to send such signals are serious about settlement. Mediators should encourage hosts to consider which rooms are appropriate for a mediation and how the accommodation will be perceived.

On-site mediations

Sometimes, the best place to mediate is on site. This maybe particularly so in neighbour and property disputes. Consideration will need to be given to what people will wear and what will happen if the weather is inclement. Again, checks will be needed to ensure that there sufficient space for everyone. In neighbour cases, the location of the plenary session will be important. These and other issues can be covered in the *mediation email* that is sometimes sent. An example is at Appendix 1.

The mediator had them all tethered for their own safety during their inflated opening statements.

Chapter 7: Who Attends the Mediation?

Introduction

There are no rules on attendance at mediation. This is a matter for the participants and it is endlessly variable. Mediators often seek to find out names and roles, or at least the numbers of the participants, beforehand – as much for housekeeping as for process. This is reflected in the draft mediation email in Appendix 1.

Who should not attend?

Drunks, those with weapons, children with no relevant interest, those with a drug or other psychosis, babes in arms, and brass bands are all regarded as being less useful than others at mediation: but remarkably, all have been experienced in different settings by mediators. Mediators are generally prepared to work with anyone who does not subvert or disrupt the process and is not obviously lacking capacity. Careful and considerate pre-mediation meetings, in private rooms, may be held to resolve these issues.

Who should attend?

Essentially mediators will ensure that those who do attend as participants in the mediation have authority to settle the claim. It is not considered good mediation practice or good faith to send a lawyer with limited (or no direct) authority who may have to spend considerable time tracking down an insurer, director, or representative of their principal who was supposed to be instantly available on the telephone.

Without such an arrangement there may well be the need for a mini-mediation between counsel/solicitor and the authorised person on the other end of the telephone, where the latter may well find it difficult to understand, by not being present, just what it is about the case that has emerged at mediation that means that previous advice and reserving or planning needs to be altered or exceeded. It will also frustrate the process if those attending mediation cannot get instructions because the organisation begins its Easter break at midday, just 90 minutes into the mediation. It has happened

Equally, it is important that the claimant attends and is not simply available by telephone: unless clinically (or exceptionally, geographically) there is no other option It is remarkably difficult to settle a claim without the beneficiary being present no matter how wide the authority given to a solicitor. If necessary, where a person has moved abroad, or is unable to travel, it is often preferable to set up a link using a video service or *Skype* or *FaceTime* or a similar webcam system rather than a pure telephone call.

If that cannot be done, and the claimant is, for example, in Kiev then consideration must also be given to Ukrainian translation and to the means of identifying the claimant to ensure that the actual client is present. Liaison with a local law firm may be necessary.

Generally, most mediators welcome the attendance of a spouse, partner, or a particular friend or family member to provide moral support, and a non-legal, common sense perspective on the process. If such a person attends, it is important to ensure that they sign the confidentiality clause appended to the Mediation Agreement[46]. It is also generally the case that both the mediator and the other party have a right (under many Mediation Agreements) to exclude persons other than the claimant and legal advisers from proceedings. In practice, for instance in clinical negligence cases, this is rarely applied – the exceptions are where there is a clear conflict of interest or undue disruption.

If a participant is a child or patient, (*a protected party* under the Civil Procedure Rules) then their duly appointed legal advisor will be required to attend the mediation. It is important that such a mediation is conducted on the understanding common to all present (and reflected in any settlement as well as the Mediation Agreement) that any agreement reached is subject to approval by the District Judge under CPR Rule 21.10.

Participants may wish to give consideration to how any agreement reached at mediation might be secured to avoid the situation in which the child claimant found himself in Drinkall v Whitwood[47] where the defendant resiled before it had been approved by the court.

Legal Advisors

Many participants in a mediation will have their legal advisors present. Where proportionate, solicitors instructed by either party may also engage counsel to attend. If they do, it will usually be appropriate to ascertain whether counsel is experienced in mediation advocacy which is, as will be apparent from what is said in Chapter 1 and in Appendix 5, a very different skill to scoring points in court. Numerous courses are available for advocates likely to work at mediation, both in-house, and as generic training. Most of the accredited providers at Appendix 7 offer such training.

[46] See Appendix 1
[47] [2003] EWCA Civ 1547

Other attendees

Defending participants' representatives may find it appropriate to bring a representative for the organisation being pursued or their insurer. Sometimes where it is thought that a direct explanation or apology is appropriate, this may include the professional under challenge. Further attendees also may include a Risk Manager or other management representative, or even company directors from the firm being pursued.

The multiplicity of potential attendees means that the arrangement of a date for the mediation, and indeed a location, can be a challenge. Most CMC Accredited Mediation Providers[48] will have a registrar who will undertake the liaison to facilitate this task.

Witnesses (other than the claimant) and experts do not normally attend mediations. Occasionally, however, participants have found it convenient to ask the experts to meet to prepare a joint statement at or before the mediation – and then take the process on from that point. This will be an uncontrollable and therefore risky strategy, however, and may require a defending participant to be very sure that there is sufficient flexibility in the settlement authority present to deal with any necessary adjustment to the case.

[48] See Appendix 2 for a list

Having pulled an all-nighter, Gonzalez, Kaminsky and Smith were exceptionally well-prepared for the mediation, but...

Chapter 8: How Should Participants Prepare?

Introduction

Effective mediation on the part of participants begins early and is a continually evolving process. Mediators report substantial differences between legal advisors and there are enormous gains to be made by apposite and complete preparation. Guidelines for advocates, including useful matters to consider in this preparation phase, are set out in Appendix 5. The remainder of this chapter considers some of the other key points.

Signing the Mediation Agreement

Before the mediation starts, the mediator will ensure that each participant has signed the Mediation Agreement (an example of which is at Appendix 1). The mediator will also sign it. This may be done before the mediation day: if not it will be done on the day of the mediation, before the mediation starts.

The mediator will also consider if there are other people attending the mediation who are not participants who will need to sign a Confidentiality Agreement.

Mediation is not a mini trial

Mediation is a facilitated negotiation. Accordingly, the participants do not usually need to bring to the mediation all of the papers, or even the evidence, they would need for a trial. Mediation can, and often does, take place before final evidence is available. There needs to be sufficient up to date evidence for participants to make settlement decisions.

The mediator will at most only need the documents that relate to the matters being mediated. Mediators will read everything that they are sent and can be expected to be familiar with it, whether it is ultimately relevant or not

Sophisticated participants recognise that the mediation is about persuading their opponents, not the mediator. It will not be possible to get the mediator on their side. They will therefore need to marshal their arguments, best points, and defences for that exercise in persuasion. Masters of the process frequently attend, or have their legal advisors attend, the opening plenary session with little or no papers at all: and will focus on what they see as the most promising lines for achieving what their clients really want out of the process, having considered carefully with them what their underlying interests are. This is a very different process to establishing or advising on their legal rights, even less carrying these through to court.

Paying the mediator

The Mediation Agreement will usually stipulate that the mediator's fee will be paid in advance of the mediation day. The general rule is that unless one participant agrees to meet the whole of the fee, the fee will be shared equally between the participants. There may be cancellation clauses as the mediation day approaches; generally, the later the cancellation, the smaller the part of fee which will be returned.

Preparation as an advocate or legal adviser

The guidelines in Appendix 5 are a useful outline. There are too excellent textbooks for guidance such as *Mediation: The Roles of Advocate and Neutral*[49] and *Mediation Representation*[50].

These encourage legal advisors to know their case and know their client. They invite advisors to be wholly familiar with the documents presented to the mediator in the mediation "bundle" or file. Legal advisors should know what is important to their client and why.

The authors encourage legal advisors to be fully familiar with their duties of good faith, the relevant code of conduct (for example, see Appendix 4) and the Mediation Agreement.

So far as the perspective of mediation is concerned, advocates and advisors should endeavour in advance to consider matters from their opponent's perspective. What would the advocate do in their opponent's shoes? They should carefully consider the weakness in their case and the strength of the opponent's case; and whether anyone else, such as an indemnity insurer, needs to be either brought to the mediation or consulted at any stage during the mediation. They should consider what offer if made would put their client at risk – how would it look and be framed?

[49] Golann & Fohlberg, Second Edition 2010 (ISBN-13: 978-0735599680)
[50] Harold Abramson, Second Edition 2011 (ISBN: 9780199693122)

Legal advisors should consider what the costs are to date and what further costs there will be to issue the claim, or go forward to trial if the matter does not resolve. They should be familiar too with what further steps may need to be taken before trial and how long they might take.

Preparing lay participants

Careful briefing of lay participants at mediation by their advisors is essential. They should know that mediation is an informal process and that they may leave at any stage if they feel it is not working for them. But they should question any such resolve to see if there is likely to be a better opportunity and the extent to which delay, hassle, and cost inform their thinking. Legal advisors should reassure clients that any decision-making will be theirs and theirs alone. As such, participants are empowered by the mediation process. They may wish to say their piece in open session. Advisors should brief them that whilst the mediation is confidential and without prejudice, anything that is said in open/plenary session is then within their opponent's knowledge and whilst they cannot refer to what was said in the mediation, they can use the information, if there is no settlement, to make further inquiries or gather further evidence.

Legal advisors and their clients should agree whether to speak in the open session and if so, who will speak and what each will say. They should decide what to do if each is asked questions by either the mediator or their opponent in the open/plenary session. They do not have to answer any questions. But how will that look? How will they decide whether to answer them? Will they need to effect a break to discuss matters privately before responding?

Written skeleton arguments for the mediator

Participants do not *have* to prepare anything: it is their process. Many people find, however, that a well prepared written skeleton argument or a mediation statement for the mediator can be helpful. These are private and confidential for the mediator only, and some mediators will shred them and not bring them to the mediation to avoid the risk of inadvertent disclosure.

Such documents can save a lot of time on the day of the mediation if they are candid and thereby have fully briefed the mediator about the priorities, concerns, needs, or interests of their client. These may of course change at the mediation if the participant discovers something they had not previously been appreciated. For this reason, mediators generally will not ask for the *bottom line*.

Dealing with costs

Mediators are prepared to assist participants deal with costs. This is something that is usually considered before the mediation as some parties will instruct specialist cost lawyers and wish to leave legal costs for another day. If costs are on the agenda, and the matter settles, then the mediator may offer to moderate discussions between the legal teams, if any, about costs. Generally, costs are agreed after the settlement has been achieved. Sometimes, however, costs are the real problem for the paying party and these are dealt with ahead of the process. Equally, global offers covering costs and damages may be made and participants should consider their responses to such tactics.

In summary

Skilled legal advisors, and mediators who see them in action, know the value of preparation. They should ensure that participants appreciate the difference time spent in preparation can make both at the mediation and in any resulting resolution.

Everyone sensed that the mediator wasn't simply giving another phony deadline.

©CharlesFincher12.28 Scribble-in-Law at LawComix.com

Chapter 9: Mediation Tactics

Introduction

This Chapter should be read in conjunction with Chapter 8. It is no substitute for experience and training, but intended as a primer by way of answering FAQs that those participants and practitioners new to mediation often pose.

Q1 What can I send the mediator?

You can send the mediator anything that you think will be helpful. You can send an agreed mediation bundle compiled with agreement of your opponent, or you can each send a set of documents to the mediator that are not agreed.

You can send a summary of issues agreed and issues in dispute, compiled with the agreement of your opponent, or you can send a confidential position statement to the mediator, for the mediator's eyes only.

Q2 What can I send the other side?

Before the mediation, you may wish to show relevant documents to your opponent in order that they may read them before the mediation. You may wish to send a position statement to them setting out your case. You may wish to refer them to relevant case law. Or you may wish to send them nothing at all.

Q3 Should a participant go into the open session?

Generally, all of the participants will go into one room with the mediator for the opening session. There the mediator will remind them of his role and the purpose of the mediation and ask them to adopt any rules that may be useful in the mediation.

The opening session starts with the housekeeping instructions, then the process is explained, then the participants are invited in turn to say anything they wish to say to one another face to face. The mediator will listen, may ask questions in clarification and will then agree the way forward for the mediation process with the participants.

Some participants refuse to go into open session initially, or there may be very good reasons why they cannot go into private session, such as an injunction. If there is a particular reason why a participant feels they do not wish to go into the open session, then discuss this with the mediator beforehand. The mediator may be able to allay any fears or concerns, or will be able to advise alternative techniques to start the mediation, such as housekeeping and opening statements in private in each participant's room. Legal advisors may consider it totally inappropriate for their client to go into the open session, for example, where they lack capacity.

Q4 Should a legal advisor let a client participant speak?

Yes, but do make sure that you have discussed what they intend to say beforehand! The mediation day is often seen by lay clients as the equivalent of their day in court. It can be a very cathartic process for them to finally be able to say how they feel about the dispute. Sometimes clients get very emotional, others may be intimidated speaking to an audience of professionals. Where there is an ongoing relationship, where trust has been eroded, or dialogue has broken down, the open session can form a crucial part of the transformative process of rebuilding trust or restoring confidence.

Q5 Must all questions be answered?

There is no requirement to answer any questions that are posed to you, or indeed by you in open session. Mediation is not about rehearsing the evidence or cross examining a witness. It is about finding a resolution that is good enough on the day. You should though consider whether it would assist the process of negotiation not to answer questions. You should not feel pressurised to answer questions when they are asked, and might prefer to take time out of the open session to discuss privately the questions raised and how to respond to them.

Q6 Is there any value in making an apology?

In many mediations, there is the opportunity to make an apology. An apology can often transform the approach to the mediation. It can be a valuable foundation to lay which will then set the tone for the negotiations. If it is to be made its implications should be considered and its tone carefully judged, and the appropriate person - participant or advisor - to deliver it chosen.

Q7 How to behave?

There are no rules in mediation, save those that the participants agree to adopt. Most advisors will of course have their own professional ethics to consider. These are set out in Appendix 5 in some detail. Generally, advocates and participants dress and behave in a business-like fashion. It may not serve either you or your client to behave or dress in an unconventional manner.

Q8 Can new evidence be disclosed at the mediation?

You can disclose whatever you think will assist the negotiations at the mediation. You will have to consider the status of that evidence once disclosed. If it is your intention to disclose the evidence for the purposes of the mediation only, then consider what the status of that document will be if the dispute is not settled at mediation? Depending upon the timing of the case there may also be a requirement for disclosure outside of the mediation.

Although the mediation is confidential and without prejudice, anything learned in the mediation will obviously be in your opponent's knowledge if the dispute does not resolve at mediation, with the consequence that they may make further inquiries and obtain further evidence themselves after the mediation.

Q9 Can surveillance evidence be disclosed at the mediation?

Yes, but do make sure that there are facilities to view it at the mediation venue. Consider also if and how it will assist the case. Once alerted to surveillance, in the event that the dispute does not settle at mediation, it may be worth considering whether opportunities to obtain further surveillance evidence will be lost.

On the other hand, surveillance evidence may be just the reality check that an opponent needs in order to settle.

Q10 Can case law be cited?

Yes, as long as it is ethical and useful in promoting a settlement. If you consider that your opponent has simply not grasped the law, or that it has not been shared with the lay client, it may be useful to refer to statutes, case law, or policies. Mediators are not there to be persuaded, however, and while they may be interested in the law, or your interpretation, it will be from the perspective of how you propose to use it as a tool to unlock the impasse rather than to assess its merits.

Q11 How about staging or threatening a walk out?

Consider how either tactic would help with the mediation? What will you do if the result is the other participant saying, 'Oh well, we had better call it a day then?' If you stage a walk out, you may in fact bring the mediation to an end.

Q12 How about complaining about the other side's behaviour?

It's possible. If there are any concerns, they should first be raised with the mediator with the request that these concerns be raised with the other side. Remember the mediator is there to encourage principled negotiation, not to act as a referee or to impose any sanctions. You might ask yourself why the other side is misbehaving and what they hope to achieve by so doing.

Q13 Can the mediation be ended anytime?

Mediation is a voluntary, consensual process. If at any stage any of those involved feel that it is not working to their advantage they can leave. Once again, they should ask themselves why it is not working and what would it take to make it work. They should also ask whether a further hour or so now may save a year or so later. The mediator will explore any reasons for wanting to leave, and see if there are reasons to encourage staying in the process. It may be that the mediator knows, but cannot tell you as yet, that there is about to be a breakthrough.

Q13 Is there any further reading on tactics that might be useful?

There are many excellent works on mediation tactics including chapters in the 2011 edition of *ADR Principles & Practice*[51] but an article written by a non-lawyer mediator *The Subversive Lawyers Guide to Mediation* by David Richbell[52] (December 2005) with its acknowledgement to Jeff Kichaven for his article *Six ways to sabotage a Mediation* (September 2005) has been well received. Its nature is summed up in the title and in the introduction:

---

[51] *Supra*

[52] http://mataw.essentialsystems.co.uk/wp-content/uploads/2010/06/the-subversive.pdf

"Mediation poses many challenges to the subversive lawyer, not least the fact that no self-respecting fee earner wants a quick and cost effective process leading to early settlement, let alone having the power and control wrested away and given to the person least equipped to handle them – the client! After all, everyone knows that ADR means Alarming Drop in Revenue."

After 16 hours of mediation, either the mediator was morphing into a strange predator or mass hallucinations had set in.

©10CharlesFincher11.04 Scribble-In-Law.com

Chapter 10: How Long Does Mediation Take?

Introduction

It is trite but true that different mediations will inevitably take different lengths of time. Some settle in 20 minutes with scarcely a word from the mediator, some break up and fail in much the same time. Some never get going at all, either because the participants agree terms in reception or because someone is ill, or ill-inclined, to go through with the process.

Time may vary with the complexity of the matter, the issues that the participants say they wish to mediate, the volume of documents, and the number of people attending the mediation. Even so, there are many surprises: a mediation about two workers wanting the same afternoon off has lasted longer than one resolving a tanker accident at sea. This chapter therefore offers a basic and inevitably subjective guide to some of the types of facilitative mediation and the typical durations for each genre.

Community Mediation
(See Chapter 12)

There are a truly vast yet largely hidden amount of community mediations, involving hundreds of groups and thousands of mediators, taking place over a whole range of disputes across the country. Most community mediation providers either operate as a charity or provide mediations to the participants free of charge, being themselves participant[aid for by local government agencies rather than private donations. Community mediations are usually done as co-mediations with two mediators working together at all times. Generally, there are no legal representatives in community mediations, and often the participants will not have taken legal advice.

Usually, the mediators or the mediation providers will have had pre-meetings with each participant before the mediation day. These will vary in length dependant upon the dispute and the vulnerability of the participants. The purpose of the pre-meetings is to explore matters from the perspective of each participant and to prepare them for the mediation. The pre-meetings may take only a few minutes, or there may be several pre-meetings taking up to an hour or so. The mediation itself will generally take between two hours and a day, depending on the conflict. There may be follow up meetings by the mediators to ensure implementation of the agreed solution.

Family Mediation

(See Chapter 13)

A wide range of family matters are mediated, including ancillary relief and matters involving children. Family mediations can take anywhere between two hours and two months, over a range of sessions, depending on the nature of the conflict. Much more information is available on the website of the Family Mediation Council, www.familymediationcouncil.org and numerous providers doing challenging work.

Small Claims Mediation

The Small Claims Mediation Service run by HM Courts and Tribunals Service is an award-winning scheme that is being redeveloped to cope with the challenges of what appears likely to become compulsory mediation in matters worth less than £10,000. These Small Claims, which for many participants still a substantial sum, generally do not involve lawyers and do not tie up judges and court time – largely the thinking behind the expansion of the concept. HMCTS presently provide their mediations free of charge.

The great majority of small claims mediations take place by telephone. In the order of 28,000 small claims mediations took place between March 2012 and March 2013. Typically, small claims mediations take between twenty minutes and two hours.

More information on this service can be found at www.civilmediation.org/downloads-get?id=482 where the HMCTS Analysis of Qualitative data is provided.

Personal Injury Mediation

Personal injury claims are now frequently mediated. Typically fast track claims are mediated in two hours. Multi track claims are being mediated in four to six hours. A specialist personal injury service for complex cases has been running for five years. More details can be found at www.trustmediation.org.uk.

Civil and Commercial Mediation

The precise volume of civil and commercial mediations is not known. Over 8,000 civil and commercial mediations were reported to the Civil Mediation Council in 2012 during its annual mediation count. The count is based on feedback from mediators and mediation providers who chose to report the number of mediations they had undertaken and is likely to be a substantial underestimate of the actual number of civil and commercial mediations that actually took place. Mediations vary in length. Fifteen years ago CEDR reported that 84% of its mediations settled in an average of 1.6 days. ADR Chambers reported in 2004 that 85% of its mediations settled in an average of seven hours and by 2009 Clerksroom was reported similar rates of settlement in around six hours.

Co-mediations, with a large number of participants have taken more than three days on some occasions, and much longer in some strategic mediations of high value and importance.

Of course even the longest mediations take a mere fraction of the time taken by a Court action.

Special Education Needs and Disability Mediation

Mediations in the educational sector are on the increase, particularly in the area of Special Educational Needs and Disability following the Equality Act 2010. Typically, SEN and Disability mediations take between two to four hours in a quiet, local, neutral venue. There are local and regional SEN mediation services and guidance on their work, methods, and contacts can be found at www.justice.gov.uk/tribunals/send/appeals/mediation while as an example of one local provider www.kids.org.uk/information/100885/100924/mediation is an accredited provider specialising in this field.

*The mediator led the group through ballet moves as a
stress-relief exercise except for Bob whose firm had
a rule against dancing at work.*

Chapter 11: Workplace and Employment Mediation

Introduction

Workplace and employment mediation have a good deal in common with civil and commercial mediation; they are both under the umbrella of the Civil Mediation Council, and many of the skills deployed are identical. There are, however, differences of procedure, emphasis, and conclusion which mean that most mediators in this work have undergone special training. This chapter is intended to provide an insight to those working in the field but is no substitute for a full course.

Workplace and Employment Mediation compared

Workplace Mediation is conducted when there is a continuing employment relationship, albeit potentially fragile or fraught.

Employment Mediation is conducted when an employee has left the employer, or is in the course of departing for a range of reasons.

A Workplace Mediation is generally instigated by the HR department, or its equivalent, which will usually be responsible for the mediator's fee. Generally, to ensure confidentiality, workplace mediations are held in a neutral venue. Usually, there are initial meetings with the HR department, followed by pre-meetings with the various stakeholders, then the mediation itself, and mediator follow up. There may also be agreement to involve other professionals.

An Employment Mediation will generally involve lawyers and there will inevitably be legal costs incurred.

Stakeholders in Workplace Mediation

There are a range of stakeholders in Workplace Mediation which include the complainant, the respondent, HR, line manager, colleagues, and Directors, and may include Unions, Occupational Health and other medical professionals. Families and colleagues may further be involved in different capacities.

Background

It is useful to understand how workplace and employment mediation has developed, to understand the current climate of change, and the changing workplace.

In 2001 the Government published *Routes to Resolution: Improving Dispute Resolution in Britain*, which led to the Employment Act of 2002. The objective was to reduce the number of grievance cases but by October 2004 it was clear that the growth of grievance cases was continuing unabated.

In 2006 the Government published *Success at Work: Protecting Vulnerable Workers, Supporting Good Employers*.

In 2007 we had the Gibbons Review, *Better Dispute Resolution: A review of employment dispute resolution in Britain*, which led to the Employment Act of 2008.

In 2009 the Business Enterprise and Regulatory Reform (BERR) published *Avoiding and Resolving Discipline and Grievance at Work*. BERR's view was that employers and employees should always try to resolve problems in the workplace at the earliest possible opportunity and usually with the least formality. ACAS agreed and revised it Code accordingly.

In 2011, the Department for Business, Innovation and Skills (BIS) and the Tribunals Service conducted a consultation and subsequently published it's 'Resolving Workplace Disputes' paper.

The present mindset

In 2008 the Chartered Institute of Personnel Development (CIPD) conducted a Workplace Mediation Survey which indicated that about 13% of medium to large organisations had a stand-alone mediation policy, but most linked it with their Discipline and Grievance policies.

The Employment Act 2009 brought the introduction of mandatory mediation in employment claims. By 2011, the Advisory, Conciliation and Arbitration Service (ACAS)

Thematic Review of Workplace Mediation concluded that there had been no change in procedure in response to the Act. Mediation was seen as just another tool that HR can use to settle disputes. The ACAS Code sets out good practice for employers and employees in dealing with disciplinary matters and grievances. It states that employers and employees should raise and deal with issues promptly and should not unreasonably delay meetings, decisions and confirmation of these decisions.

Employers and employees should act consistently. Employers should carry out any necessary investigations, to establish the facts of the case. Employers should inform employees of the basis of the problem and give them an opportunity to put their case in response before any decisions are made. Employers should allow employees to be accompanied at any disciplinary or grievance hearing. Employers should allow an employee to appeal against any formal decision made.

The business case for mediation

In 2008 it was estimated by the Office for national Statistics and the CIPD that workplace conflict costs the UK economy more than £24 billion. 370 million working days were lost in the UK in 2007 alone.

A study at East Sussex County Council estimated that raising a grievance to board level through the Right of Appeal process resulted in 32 days of HR case management, similar time for the unions, 10 to 12 days work by the legal department and over 32 days line manager input. In contrast, mediation involved a total 3 days; one day of preparation, one day for mediation and one day follow-up. The conservative estimate of loss of productivity or efficiency, based on an average salary of £27,000, amounted to £500,000 per case studied. With a typical Employment Tribunal case costing £18,000 and a typical mediation costing £2,500 the cost argument for mediation is clear.

Consequently, for many businesses there is a direct profitability link between the cost of workplace disputes being resolved by the cumbersome traditionally process and mediation Mediation in the workplace and in employment matters is found to be cost and resource effective, with the overwhelming number of disputes being resolved in the process.

Causes of conflict in the workplace

Studies have looked at a wide range of causes of conflict, almost all of which are found to be well suited to resolution though workplace mediation. The surveys suggest that the following elements are present in cases of conflict:

Personality clashes and warring egos	49%
Stress	34%
Heavy workloads and inadequate resources	33%
Poor leadership from the top	29%
Lack of honesty and openness	26%
Poor line management.	23%
Lack of role clarity.	22%
Lack of clarity about accountability.	21%
Clash of values.	18%
Poor selection and pairing of teams	16%
Taboo subjects e.g. office affairs	15%
Poor performance management	14%
Bullying and harassment	13%
Perceived discrimination	10%

Mediator follow up

Civil and commercial mediations are more defined in terms of timescale than Workplace Mediations. Workplace follow-up is integral part of the process in Workplace Mediations. People are often on an emotional journey and need time to rebuild trust or lost confidence. A follow-up plan may then be agreed with the HR department and participants, and this plan may need to deal with behavioural change. Working with the HR departments and line managers on a confidential basis, the mediator may identify the need for coaching, psychotherapy, mentoring, training and development, counselling or occupational health.

The mechanisms for sharing these will need to be covered in the Mediation Agreement which will have been carefully prepared.

Confidentiality

The Mediation Agreement in Workplace Mediation accordingly varies slightly from the civil and commercial Mediation Agreement because of the nature of the engagement of the mediator by the HR department. Of necessity, there will be a requirement for the mediator to feed back certain information to the HR department. There are also some boundaries in the mediator's confidentiality where, for example, the mediator becomes aware of a breach of the employment contract, or information is revealed of illegal activity, or activity that is likely to cause serious harm to an employee.

Power imbalances

Workplace mediators are aware of the potential for power imbalances to arise in Workplace Mediation and have a range of skills and tactics to ensure that there is a fair and balanced opportunity for people to discuss matters in a non-judgmental way and in confidence. There may be a feeling of intimidation on the part of an employee or fear of losing their job. It can be very intimidating process for an employee to engage in discussions about other employees, and particularly if there is a complaint or allegations against a line manager or senior member of staff. In some cases, trust may be so badly eroded, that it takes a number of pre-meetings before the mediator is able to commence the mediation proper.

Compromise Agreements and Settlements

In a Workplace Mediation, where a resolution is reached, the terms will usually be reduced to writing and signed. In Employment Mediations and some Workplace Mediations, a Compromise Agreement is required, for example, where there is a termination of the employment contract, a payment by the employer in exchange for an agreement by the employee to waive the right to pursue specified existing or future employment tribunal claims, or a variation in the terms and conditions of employment. The Compromise Agreement may be in the form of a COT[53], involving an ACAS conciliator. The agreement may be a bespoke, drafted Compromise Agreement. This will require legal input on the part of the employer, and the complainant must take independent legal advice on the agreement before signing it.

[53] An ACAS formal document or compromise procedure

The employer usually agrees to pay for the complainant to obtain independent legal advice before signing the Compromise Agreement. There may be a cap of the sum agreed. Typically the employer will agree to pay £250-500. Any agreement reached may be void in the absence of independent legal advice.

Mediators and participants should be aware that some specialist knowledge and careful thought may be needed to avoid future problems. The Law Society issued guidance on compromise agreements which can be found at www.lawsociety.org.uk/advice/practice-notes/compromise-section-147. The ACAS guidance can be found at www.acas.org.uk/index.aspx?articleid=2006.

In summary

Workplace and Employment Mediation is set to become of much greater importance over the coming years. There are significant differences in process between the two and civil and commercial mediation but many mediators make the conversion with additional training and find the work worthwhile and important. Mediation is an important option for all practitioners working in the law regarding workers and employees to be fully are of, and to use.

Margaret's skills as a peacemaker had exceeded expectations at the mediaton.

Chapter 12: Community Mediation

Introduction

Community Mediation (CM) brings the restorative principle into the world of neighbour and community conflict. As with most forms of mediation it is a 'no blame' intervention.

Many CM organisations sprang up in the 1980s and 90s under the umbrella of Mediation UK to help neighbours address their disagreements without recourse to the police or the civil courts. In spite of the demise of Mediation UK in 2006 and difficulties of financial viability, many CM organisations have survived – and some thrived – so that a reasonable proportion of the population of the United Kingdom still has access to a CM service.

This chapter will give an overview of how services are funded and supported, who the referrers are, who uses the service and why, who mediates and how they are selected and trained, what the process is and who benefits and how.

Who funds?

The main funders for CM services have been local authorities, who as providers of large-scale public housing have had a natural stake in neighbour conflict resolution. Housing associations and the police have played a part while charitable grants and local fundraising have also contributed.

Some organisations self-generate all or part of their income through the sale of their services. Most CM organisations are registered charities whilst some are in-house services within local authorities. Virtually all deliver the service free at the point of use.

Many charity and local authority grants have been reduced or withdrawn over times of financial constraint so that service deliverers have increasingly to bid for service level agreements with local authorities and housing associations to survive and to continue to deliver a free service to householders.

Additionally, there are a very few private companies offering CM.

Who refers?

In some areas the majority of CM cases are referred by local authorities and housing associations in relation to disputes between residents in their housing stock. They may have an agreement to refer a maximum number of cases per year or they may make ad hoc referrals. In other places the police, who are frequently called to non-criminal neighbour disputes and incidents of anti-social behaviour, also may refer.

Many other cases are self-referred, prompted by publicity or via advice agencies such as the Citizens' Advice Bureau. Increasingly main referrers are trained to refer appropriately and to deal initially with residents in a way that is in accord with mediation principles.

Who uses CM and why?

Most users of CM are living in public housing where population concentration is high, although cases also come from the privately owned and rented sectors. Particular issues can arise where council houses have been bought alongside those still rented.

Some referrals come from within a household, for example where intergenerational conflict may lead to young people being threatened with homelessness.

CM may also deal with conflict arising in residential settings such as children's homes, retirement or assisted living communities or between children, parents and teachers in a school community. Common issues resolved by CM include noise, aggression, parking, children's behaviour, offensive language, animals, rubbish, trees, hedges, and boundaries. Underlying issues often concern cultural, age and attitude differences, drugs, alcohol, and mental and physical health. Fears often concern eviction, loss of house value, loss of respect, health, choice or privacy and sometimes real fear of physical harm.

Who mediates?

Most Community Mediators are volunteers and are only paid for the expenses of administration and travel. They usually work in pairs. Mediators may be from any background and are often recruited through local advertising. There may be a system of selection before training as well as after it. It is often the case that there is a degree of self-regulation; people who are not very competent tend not to enjoy the training or the practice and drift away.

Who trains?

In the past Mediation UK designed and ran training courses for mediators but since its demise organisations have had to create their own courses, often based on the Mediation UK model, approved and accredited by such bodies as the Open College Network.

Typically the course would be a six-day course in basic mediation skills with an emphasis on Community Mediation. Most services provide support and continuing development for mediators with ongoing training and supervision by experienced mediators or by peer supervision.

How does it work?

Mediators will usually be given a brief outline of the problem by the referrer or by a model known as Assessment Mediation. Her, both parties are visited by an Assessor who discusses the issues in a restorative way (asking what happened? How were you affected? What needs to happen for you to move forward?) but may be more robust than a traditional mediator in signposting other agencies, encouraging reality checking, challenging unrealistic expectations and giving advice. This model is popular with housing authorities as it leaves housing officers free to deal with the very small percentage of intractable cases returned to them.

When appropriate the Assessor will suggest and arrange a mediation, which is then undertaken by volunteer mediators at a local but neutral venue. There the participants will give them an opportunity to talk about what has happened and how they feel, help them to identify the current issues and think about possible ways forward. Everyone will be given uninterrupted time to talk about what has happened and how they have been affected and in a managed discussion will hope to move on to agree a way forward which is achievable, proportionate, specific and time-structured.

A written agreement may be drawn up and signed (some referrers require this) and whilst it is not a legally binding document it is a useful reminder for both neighbours of what they have decided.

There is generally a high level of confidentiality on the part of mediators although some referrers expect a report. Participants will always be told if this is the case. They may ask that some information is kept confidential and this would normally be agreed unless serious crime or harm to children were involved.

There may be power imbalances at a face to face meeting and, for example, a single neighbour meeting a couple may be asked if they would like to bring a friend or family member for support. Personality imbalances should be dealt with by good management of the process. Racial or gender prejudice would usually be challenged by mediators and if very entrenched may make mediation inappropriate.

Where neighbours are unwilling to meet a shuttle mediation may be conducted but tends to have more limited success. Experience suggests that where neighbours can be brought face to face an agreement is reached in 90% of cases.

Whilst the most common mediation will be between two households of one or two people, there are other models. A larger group of neighbours from several households, for example, may meet for a conference. As this is still treated as a 'no blame' meeting it can be complex, time consuming and demanding to manage.

Is there any follow-up?

Most organisations will offer follow-up help after a mediation, inviting participants to get in touch if they need to. Some mediators make contact after a period of time. The most important factor, it is reported, is the availability and confidence in the process of mediation. Others believe it can be detrimental to do follow up, fearing it may rekindle problems.

Who benefits?

The obvious beneficiaries are the residents who have often been trapped in troubled relationships with neighbours. Reports to police or housing officers may have failed and they cannot easily resolve the conflict themselves without impartial help.

Mediators keep discussions calm, witness what is said, help identify real issues and separate them from those which are historic or relatively unimportant, allow feelings to be expressed but not to dominate, encourage practical strategies for living alongside each other and help participants to feel empowered to deal with their own differences in the future. Communities benefit in that the ripple effects and polarisations surrounding a dispute are defused and over time the idea is sown that people can deal with their own conflicts within a community. The widely held attitude of, 'We've got a problem, who's going to solve it?' can be shifted to, 'We've got a problem, what can we do about it?'

Local authorities, housing associations and the police benefit in the saving of time and resources and ultimately hard cash. Their outlay in buying in CM represents excellent value for money, costs reflecting the not-for-profit nature and volunteer workforce of most services. Sadly, in the current climate of austerity, short-term savings are often chosen over longer-term benefit. Reductions in cost to the health service, social services and criminal justice system are harder to quantify but improvements in well-being and reduction in crime are undoubted spin-offs of CM.

Formal evaluation of CM's effectiveness has not been consistent or easy to research. An agreement is usually deemed successful if there is no further complaint to the referrer within a period of six months. However this is only a partial indicator of success from the point of view of the parties involved.

Where are we now?

With rising concern at many levels about anti-social behaviour and a fear of perceived crime in our communities, as well as the continuing conflicts arising between neighbours, the need for CM is as great as ever.

The use of mediation is now mandatory in many other fields as a diversion from precipitous court action. While successive governments have spoken enthusiastically about CM and identified good practice in many areas, lack of commitment to funding often hampers expansion of the work.

A divorce mediator playing with dolls.

c.07CharlesFincher03.26 Scribble-in-Law at LawComix.com

Chapter 13: Family Mediation

Introduction

Some say that family disputes are the most pernicious, difficult and abrasive matters to come to the attention of lawyers or authorities. They are almost always challenging.

Family mediation (FM) is used by couples who are either at the point of separation, or already separated or getting divorced to settle issues that might include parenting plans, financial matters, child support and maintenance or any other problem particular to their personal circumstances.

FM offers the opportunity for parents, or (former) couples, to discuss any or all of these matters together with the assistance of a mediator, or two co-mediators, to reach a jointly negotiated settlement. FM is also appropriate in other family circumstances, for example where families have a dependent adult to consider or disputes between adult siblings.

The Family Mediation Council, established in 2007, governs the training and the 2010 Code of Practice. The training and practice for FM differs from civil, commercial, workplace and employment mediation.

This chapter is intended to give an insight in to the world of FM it is not a substitute for training as a family mediator.

Origins

FM in the UK began following the recommendations of the *Finer Report on One-Parent Families* (1974) for a new system of family courts in which conciliation would be the preferred means of settling issues arising from separation and divorce.

The first FM service was started in Bristol in 1978 as a local project run by social workers and family lawyers. This pilot scheme offered mediation out of court on child related issues. Independent, out-of-court mediation developed in parallel with court directed conciliation schemes, cases where judges referred disputes over children to the divorce court welfare service The Children and Family Court Advisory and Support Service (CAFCASS).

Independent FM services, funded mainly by charitable grants, spread across Britain during the 1980s and 90s. Twenty years of campaigning for family law reform and public funding for FM services led to The Family Law Act 1996. Parts I and II of the Act – introducing a major reform of divorce law, were abandoned as unworkable. Part III of the Act dealt with FM and these provisions were implemented. Section 13 (Resolution of Disputes) sets out directions with respect to mediation. Domestic violence and other cases were exempt from the requirement to consider mediation before legal aid could be obtained. This was amended in The Access to Justice Act 1999, and the exemptions were reduced in 2007 and in November 2010.

The present government mind set

The Ministry of Justice (MoJ) in England and Wales introduced the Practice Direction 3A – Pre-Application Protocol for Mediation Information and Assessment - commonly known as MIAMs – in 2011. There is currently an expectation that before applying to the family court people will need to prove they have considered mediation first. This is done:

By showing they are exempt from having to consider mediation, for example if domestic violence is involved or;

By proving to the judge that they have been to a MIAM with a family mediator from which mediation was not deemed suitable.

It is important that people in family disputes are made aware of this. The Children and Families Bill, currently progressing through Parliament, seeks to make this a legal requirement. MoJ figures suggest the average overall cost of a mediated separation is £535 as against up to £7,000 for litigated cases. The MoJ is keen on mediation – ploughing an additional £10m in to mediation services in 2013, to bring the total annual funding to around £25m.

Changes to the legal aid system in England and Wales came in to effect in April 2013, meaning that legal aid will no longer be available for private family law cases, including child contact arrangements and anything to do with divorce. In other words, if people want to go to court from now on they will have to pay the costs or represent themselves. FM is becoming more and more attractive.

Core principles of FM

The Family Justice Council (FJC) and the Family Mediation Council (FMC) have jointly issued a document for widespread circulation, endorsed by the President of The Family Division, entitled *Independent Mediation – Information for Judges, Magistrates and Legal Admin* (2011). This document defines four core principles of FM:

> It is a voluntary process;
>
> It is a confidential process;
>
> The mediator acts in an impartial way;
>
> Decision-making rests with the participants at the mediation.

These principles will be familiar to all forms of mediators.

The formal process

The formal process is straightforward. First there is an assessment to identify key areas that need resolving, usually finance and child related. At this point a Mediation Agreement is signed if mediation is to proceed.

There then follows four or five 90-minute sessions, at two or three week intervals, for all issues to be mediated. The frequency varies with the complexity of the issues. At the end of every session the mediator(s) write up a session summary for the participants. At the end of the process a Memorandum of Understanding and an Open Financial Statement will be drafted. Although these are not legal documents in themselves, they can be taken to a solicitor and form the basis of a legal settlement.

Family mediators fully understand the law on child maintenance, on benefits, tax, pensions, wills and property. You have to know that what is suggested is legal and sustainable. Family mediators will know the Matrimonial Causes Act 1973, Matrimonial and Family Procedures Act 1984, and Family Law Act 1996, Civil Partnership Act 2004, The Children Act 1989, Child Support Act 1991 and the unmarried couples Trust of Land and Appointment of Trustees Act 1996. A family mediator's work is about finding common ground, keeping the channels open and rephrasing to take the emotion out of communications.

Co-mediation is very common in FM as it is in community and in workplace mediations. It is generally to do with gender balance so that the mediators reflect the couple. The co-mediators may be from disparate professions – legal professional with another professional working in social work or counselling or therapy – or not a professional at all. Co-mediation lessens the opportunity for triangulation and also supports one another within and outside the process.

Types of mediation used in Family Mediation

Transformative mediation skills may be used in FM as they are in employment disputes. Transformative mediation seeks fresh vision through talking and listening which empowers the couple to seek recognition. This is useful in FM as it allows each autonomy and a fresher understanding of feelings and perspectives.

Narrative mediation skills are used in family by allowing the couple to tell their story, which involves them equally and helps them to a shared understanding of the feelings between them.

Structured mediation in resolving disputes in divorce emerged from Coogler, *Structured Mediation in Divorce Settlement* and Haynes, *Divorce Mediation– A Practical Guide*. It is a staged model with balanced participation providing physical and psychology boundaries that help contain strong emotions and channel energies towards problem solving and negotiation. Shuttle mediation is more commonly used in commercial, civil and workplace mediation but can be used in FM where domestic violence has been an issue or with complex financial issues or high conflict couples. The level of confidentially is agreed in advance commonly an agreement to maintain separate confidences.

Confidentiality

The Mediation Agreement in FM varies slightly from other forms of Mediation Agreements due to finance and property disclosures which requires full and frank access to finance with supporting documentation. Financial disclosures are made on the basis that they are confidential but may be disclosed to solicitors and used as evidence in court.

Another exception to confidentiality is where there is a child or any person at risk of serious harm, in which case the mediator may contact the appropriate authorities.

Competence of mediators

Once a mediator has passed the FM course and completed 10 hours of observations then they are able to undertake private FM cases – but not publicly funded ones. In order to undertake Legal Services Commission Recognition publicly funded FM a mediator must either have;

Successfully passed the Family Mediation Councils Assessment of Professional Competence (APC) Scheme or;

Obtain a Practitioner Membership of the Law Society's Family Mediation Panel.

This will then allow the mediator to work for a publically funded franchise mediation service which has a contract from the Legal Services Commission.

All practicing family mediators have to be a member of one of the five member organisations of the Family Mediation Council and abide by their Code of Practice 2010. To become approved by those member bodies each family mediator has to have a Personal Practice Consultant know as a PPC who is a mentor.

Statistics

Office of National Statistics reported that the number of divorces in England and Wales in 2010 was 119,589, an increase of 4.9% since 2009, when there were 113,949 divorces. Furthermore, more than 40% of marriages end in divorce and one in four children will experience their parents' divorce by the age of 16.

The Divorce and Separation Outcomes for Children (Joseph Rowntree Foundation), reports that one in four children live in lone parent families and one in ten children live in a stepfamily.

In Summary

FM is already at the forefront of divorce and separation and this is set to increase. There are significant differences in process but many mediators make the conversion from civil and commercial mediation with additional training and find the work challenging and worthwhile.

Mediation is an important option for couples divorcing, separating, co-habiting or in civil partnerships. It is also an option for extended family such as grandparents.

Both sides were at a loss as to how to make their presentations if they couldn't tweet.

Chapter 14: Advocates at Mediation

Introduction

Mediation advocacy is a specialist skill. A good mediation advocate will have prepared for the mediation and will have a strategy in mind, but will also keep an open mind, as there may be unexpected developments which require them to devise and adopt a revised strategy during the mediation.

Both clients and opponents can spring surprises. A good mediation advocate will encourage their client to adopt principled negotiation and to weigh risk. They will also consider their client's needs and concerns, rather than approaching the solution from a judicial perspective.

This guidance draws on original work by the London School of Mediation, which in turn acknowledges the materials available from the UK Bar Council, the Law Society, the Standing Conference of Mediation Advocates and the Law Council of Australia.

The guidance is not definitive, nor does it have any statutory or regulatory force, but represents perceived good practice for those representing participants in the civil mediations on which this book is focussed.

The guide may also be useful for those representing themselves or acting as lay advisors in the mediation process. It does not, of course, replace in whole or in part any of the Codes of Conduct which place duties on relevant professionals such as barrister[54] or solicitors[55]. For example: under the Bar Code of Conduct (2005):

Conduct in Mediation

> 708.1 *A barrister instructed in a mediation must not knowingly or recklessly mislead the mediator or any party or their representative.*

There is no comparable provision in the 2011 Code of Conduct for solicitors published by the Solicitors Regulation Authority: indeed the word mediation does not appear in the Code or the handbook but it is right that the general duties of a solicitor will apply in mediation.

---

[54] http://www.barstandardsboard.org.uk/regulatory-requirements/the-code-of- conduct/the-code-of-conduct/part-vii-conduct-of-work-by-practising-barristers/

[55] http://www.sra.org.uk/solicitors/handbook/code/content.page

The duty of the advocate

It is the duty of the advocate to act ethically in the best interests of their client throughout the mediation and to comply with the applicable Code of Conduct.

As part of this duty the advocate should be sufficiently familiar with the mediation process, and with their instructions; and to have had adequate time to prepare themselves and their client before the mediation begins.

The role of the advocate

It is the role of the advocate (either alone or in combination with other advisors) to help their client achieve an acceptable resolution by:

- providing appropriate legal advice before and at the mediation;
- providing advice on the mediation process, before and at the mediation;
- preparing the client for the mediation including by assessing risk;
- preparing a file of appropriate documents to be sent to the mediator;
- preparing any open statement for use at the mediation;
- preparing any confidential statement to be sent to the mediator only;
- ensuring that other participants will attend with sufficient authority;
- selecting the most appropriate mediator commensurate with resources;
- ensuring the mediation agreement is signed before mediation;
- planning how and by whom their client's case should be presented;
- presenting their client's case in accordance with the plan;
- working with the mediator where that is likely to assist their client;
- advising their client whether to speak, or to answer questions;
- advising on matters discussed in or arising at mediation;
- advising on what it anything should be disclosed during the mediation;
- considering their client's interests in the light of matters learned ;
- advising on offers made or to be made, including on their presentation;

- drafting written offers to be communicated by the mediator in mediation;
- drafting or advising on any written settlement or heads of agreement; and
- drafting or advising on any offer intended to be live or survive after the mediation.

Advocates will be alive to the potentially changing nature of their client's case and interests during mediations, will consider whether the mediation process is being properly used by all concerned, and will continually monitor whether it is, or is likely to be, the most appropriate matter of obtaining what it is their client really wishes to achieve from a resolution of the dispute.

It follows that the role of the advocate is one of continuous engagement through the mediation – listening, assessing, and if appropriate, speaking either to persuade others or to assist the mediator in achieving an outcome acceptable to their client. It also follows that effective mediation advocates will have a thorough understanding of the mediation process, its opportunities and potential pitfalls, and will be able to recognise, work with and exploit the very significant differences compared to trial and arbitration advocacy.

Ethics and confidentiality

An advocate must behave ethically, both under their relevant Code of Conduct and in terms of the obligations imposed by the mediation agreement under which the mediation takes place.

An advocate should comply with any obligations and requirements imposed on them under the mediation agreement and should ensure that their clients are similarly compliant.

During the mediation, advocates and their clients should act in good faith at all times. An advocate should not act in bad faith at any time and should advise their client as to conduct which might amount to bad faith. An advocate who suspects that other participants may be acting in bad faith will consider whether to raise the suspicions with the mediator if to do so is likely to be in the best interests of their client.

Subject to the terms of any order of a court, an advocate must maintain the confidentiality required by the mediation agreement and therefore must not disclose anything said or done during the mediation unless all the participants agree.

An advocate should be familiar with the relevant local laws or rules as to the status of documents disclosed during mediation, which may vary both in different jurisdictions, and in respect of different classes of document.

Advocates must not ask the mediator to disclose information which has been given to them in private sessions (caucuses) with other participants and which the mediator has not been authorised to disclose.

Advocates should not act on or use information or documents that have been inadvertently disclosed by other participants in the mediation but should comply with their relevant duties under their Code of Conduct in respect of such a situation.

Advocates must not attempt to make an electronic or digital recording of the mediation or any part of the mediation, and should inform their clients that this is not permissible. Advocates must comply with any restrictions on note taking, or the later use of notes, that may be set out in the mediation agreement,

Conduct at the mediation

Advocates should ensure that their clients recognise that mediation is not a trial nor a determinative exercise, and that the mediator decides nothing of substance. It is one where the relevant decision maker, who may sometimes only be represented at the mediation, will need to be persuaded to resolve the matter on terms which the advocate's client can accept.

Accordingly the advocate should ensure that everything that the advocate and their client says, does, or discloses, including the manner and style of their actions, including any apology or admission, is carefully considered so as to be an effective instrument in persuasion. Language, detail, and the basis of legal technical terms should reflect the receptivity of the person to be persuaded.

Advocates should be familiar with and consider the use where appropriate of some or all of the facets of principled negotiation and/or the steps set out for example in *Getting Past No* including:

- the use of reflective language;
- going to the balcony
- reframing rather than rejection
- separating the people from the problem
- building a golden bridge
- using reason rather than threats
- stepping to their side
- understanding the interests of opponents
- turning adversaries into partners

Advocates must never knowingly or recklessly mislead in a mediation, whether in respect of facts or an offer or its terms.

Advocates must not attempt to use the mediator to transmit information, or an offer, or certain terms of the offer which the mediator knows is incorrect, or is likely to mislead, and should explain to their client why a mediator cannot so act.

Advocates should be wary of the use of bluster, puff, and hyperbole in mediation. They should generally use ordinary business language and tone.

Offers and settlement

Advocates should advise their client to be prudent in the use of language such as *bottom line* or *final offer*: advocates will wish their clients to understand that such phrases may lead to an unintended premature ending of the mediation by the other participants, and that ultimatums which can limit the scope for future negotiation or may damage credibility.

Advocates should advise their client on the likely most effective method of transmitting an offer, which at any given point in the mediation may vary. The most common methods (each of which has advantages and disadvantages) are:

- Direct by the client to the other participants in a plenary session
- Direct by the advocate to the other participants in a plenary session
- Direct by the advocate to another advocate only, with or without the mediator
- Indirectly through a written offer transmitted by the mediator
- Indirectly through an oral offer transmitted by the mediator (although recognising if they do, that this method is fraught with possibilities for mistake or interpretative error).

Advocates should continually assess the mood of the mediation and how at any time the varying options for presentation of an offer are likely to benefit their client's best interests The mediator may be willing to assist in providing an indication of whether a face to face offer or a written offer is likely to be best received by other participants.

Advocates should consider taking a number or draft printed or hand-written settlement agreements to the mediation, or whether to have a draft available digitally, which cover the main points likely to be required by their client. In so considering, advocates will have regard to the likely effect of producing a pre-prepared draft may have on the other participants who may feel that such a document suggests little movement or gain has been achieved.

Termination without settlement

In the event of a mediation not resulting in a settlement the advocate should consider whether there are matters which can be agreed to narrow the issues, and if so whether these can be reduced into writing. If an offer is left open the advocate should consider if it needs to be put in writing in order to survive confidentiality.

Support and development

Mediation advocates can gain much by training and support. The authors commend the programme offered by the Standing Conference of Mediation Advocates and its eminent coordinator Andrew Goodman. More on http://www.mediationadvocates.org.uk

Chapter 15: Conclusion

This handbook is intended to offer practical advice and as such there is much contained in both the Appendices and the Annex which will amplify what has been written and be of practical use to all parties involved in the world of mediation.

For those wishing to know more, there are a range of links in Appendix 6.

It is intended that the reader should be left with the knowledge that mediation is real, happening, practical, and worthwhile in a wide range of cases and disciplines, but that it is not a panacea for every ill.

While predictions are dangerous in the as yet undefined future of civil litigation, and there have been false dawns, it is reasonable to believe that mediation has a much greater scope than is presently being used and that it will sit well alongside joint settlement meetings, judicial decisions and the arbitration process.

It will, most observers suggest, exist in a healthy parallel role while becoming a more important tool than was imagined even five or six years ago.

Whether there will be a Mediation Act in 2018 as some have predicted remains to be seen. The European dimension may so require in due course but questions will need to be answered as to who bears the cost of any greater regulation, and who the responsibility of overseeing such changes.

But mediation and mediators perhaps should be more concerned with the micro than the macro. Mediation is for people, all sorts of people in all sorts of situations, with problems. For it is in the attitude and faces, the feedback and the realisation of satisfied participants, that many consider the future of mediation is really based. If that is right, then the process will indeed have an assured future.

For those wishing to train as mediators, whether as individuals or as part of an in-house group, the list of CMC Recognised Training Organisations is at Appendix 7.

Appendix 1: Proceeds of Crime and Money Laundering

The Civil Mediation Council and the Chartered Institute of Arbitrators have adopted identical guidance to mediators, whether lawyers or non-lawyers, on the duty of a mediator in respect of the Proceeds of Crime Act 2002.

It is an important subject and the attention of practitioners is drawn to the guidance which is found at: http://www.ciarb.org/information-and-resources/practice-guidelines-and-protocols/list-of-guidelines-and-protocols/.

The CMC Board had, in 2010, been told that one mediation provider was still including in its Standard Mediation Agreement a clause to the effect that

> "...the mediator has an absolute obligation under the Proceeds of Crime Act 2002 to report to the NCIS any knowledge or suspicion relating to the involvement of the proceeds of crime (including tax evasion) and is precluded by law from informing the Parties of his intention to do so."

This was certainly believed to be the effect of Part 7 of the 2002 Act when it was first enacted. Indeed, the CMC convened a Forum in December 2004 to ventilate worries about the supposed effect of the Act in this respect. In March 2005, however, the Court of Appeal gave authoritative guidance on the meaning of this part of the Act, and although its judgment was not expressly concerned with the position of mediators, it led to the Chartered Institute of Arbitrators publishing authoritative guidance on the effect of the Act for mediators, arbitrators and adjudicators.

Although the precise meaning of the Act must be a matter for the courts, the Board of the CMC believes that the Guidance has been universally followed, without any mishap, over the last five years. The force of the guidance, which should be studied by all practitioners, is that:

> "4.2.1 Bowman v Fels resolves most if not all of the problems created by POCA which can affect mediators. It follows from the decision that:
>
> (1) a mediator, whether he is a lawyer or not, will generally not be at risk of being concerned in an "arrangement", if he merely facilitates a consensual resolution of a dispute in the context of litigation;

(2) it is not necessary for litigation to have actually been commenced; see the reference to "existing or contemplated legal proceedings"; and

(3) similarly a mediator will not generally be at risk if he merely facilitates a consensual resolution of a dispute in the context of an existing or contemplated arbitration."

But the Board drew attention to the fact that the Guidance recognises that mediators may in certain circumstances incur the obligations created by the Act. It therefore encouraged all training providers, mediation providers and individual mediators to study the Guidance carefully, so as to ensure that mediators never run the risk of incurring criminal liability under the Act in any circumstances. This is a very important part of the guidance.

In particular the Guidance is noted to warn mediators that although many of their earlier worries were not substantiated by the judgment of the Court of Appeal, they should exercise care in two situations:

(a) where there are no existing or contemplated legal or arbitration proceedings or where the link between the mediation and such proceedings is tenuous;

(b) where (even if there are existing or contemplated proceedings) the settlement "[did] not reflect the legal and practical merits of the parties' respective positions in the proceedings and was known or suspected to be no more than a pretext for agreeing on the acquisition, retention, use or control of criminal property".

In the latter case the Guidance suggests that it will almost certainly be ethical for the mediator to withdraw from the mediation once suspicions of this kind are aroused.

Before withdrawing, however, it is suggested that he should give the participants the opportunity to rebut any suspicion he may hold that the mediation was being used as a pretext for agreeing on the acquisition, retention, use or control of criminal property. In parallel with the Guidance, mediators will know that their duty under both the European Code of Conduct at Appendix 4, and under most Mediation Agreements, will be to terminate a mediation if they believe that it is unethical to continue. That would certainly be the case where the mediator remained suspicious.

Appendix 2: Model Mediation Documents

Introduction

This Appendix contains a selection of sample mediation documents that may be useful reference points for practitioners. They are:

> (1) A draft (emailed) letter of invitation to mediate
>
> (2) A draft mediation agreement by which participants appoint the mediator
>
> (3) Draft mediation rules
>
> (4) A draft mediation email to actual participants from a mediator.

The first is something that may be useful in helping to persuade people to agree to mediate. Many find it more effective simply to pick up the telephone or make the suggestion in face to face discussions, but where that is not possible, or unlikely to work, the invitation letter might be considered.

The mediation agreement and rules are self-explanatory and one sample of a variety of texts used around the world. Many more can be found through a *Google* search.

The last email is one example of something used by some, but not all, mediators. They find it helpful to set out in more detail how a mediation runs to those who are likely to be unfamiliar with the process.

Important note and caveat

All of the samples should be treated as frameworks for discussion and not as definitive items ready for action: it is important that every time a document is used it should be thought about and considered for relevance and effectiveness. No warranties are offered or given as to the appropriateness or utility of any of these documents and they do not constitute advice. These documents may also time expire or become inappropriate because of changes in the law, rules, or mediation context. Prospective users must assure themselves that they are fully aware of the law, rules, and context or take professional advice on the same.

Draft Mediation Invitation E-mail/Letter

(sent on behalf of a Defendant's insurer by their solicitors)

Dear Sirs,

RE: **Mr Little Man v Giant Bus Co. Ltd (Accident 8th July 2010)**
        MEDIATION OFFER – WITHOUT PREJUDICE SAVE AS TO COSTS

Further to our recent correspondence, please note that the writer has conducted a full review of this case and discussed the matter with counsel. You will recall that this is a claim where liability is admitted and proceedings are stayed for negotiations.

We have formed the considered view that the time is right for settlement and we are pleased to make the without prejudice offer set out below. If it is rejected, which we hope it will not be, then we will rely on this letter in respect of the incidence and basis of costs, in any event.

We are instructed to offer mediation and would invite you to take instructions on meeting for mediation at a suitable venue during May 2014 without so far as possible avoiding incurring any other costs before then.

We believe that one of the following mediators would be wholly appropriate:

(a)   Ms Judith Kelbie (insurance solicitor – Judith Kelbie LLP (01423 87 4567)

(b)   Mr Jonathan Dingle (personal injury barrister – 218 Strand (01823 704072)

(c)   Sir Henry Brooke (ex-Court of Appeal judge – Trust Mediation (0207 353 3237)

We understand that they are all are former elected Board Members of the Civil Mediation Council and are all happy to discuss their general approach to approach to mediations with potential parties (bit not the detail of the case) – they are available at

(a)   Ms Kelbie   07769 176868

(b)   Mr Dingle   07771 742953

(c)   Sir Henry   0207 353 3936

We have not spoken to them ourselves about this but are happy for you to do so if you wish.

We are instructed to offer to pay all[56] of the mediator's costs of the mediation in advance on the basis that it is a recoverable disbursement in the usual way. We make it clear that other than your attendance there will be no cost to you. For reference, each of the mediators' fees is, we understand, £3,000+VAT for a six hour mediation including preparation and travel.

We are happy to hold the mediation in your offices in Sheffield or at a venue more convenient to your client to be agreed. We have done a preliminary diary check and the following dates appear clear to us –

(1)   7th May 2014   (1000 start)

(2)   19th May 2014   (1200 start)

(3)   20th May 2014   (1000 start)

We believe that four to six hours are likely to be sufficient. If necessary, all of the mediators have overtime available. Our experience is that it is unlikely.

We will attend with full authority to settle with or from our insurer client and are prepared to approach matters with an open mind using to the mediator to help us look for a solution. We think we have enough evidence and we all know what our respective experts and witnesses are likely to say. We do not need any more pleadings or papers from our perspective.

We hope that you will agree to attend with your clients. If you do, we are confident of settlement – we know that around 90% of these matters settle at mediation or shortly afterwards. Please let us know, formally or informally, your preferences to dates as soon as you can.

---

[56] Note: if this were an invitation from the Claimant the offer would usually be 50% of the costs each.

If you are minded to reject this offer then you will no doubt draw your client's attention to the authorities on costs going back as far as *Dunnett v Railtrack* and continuing through to Rolf v De Guerin [2011] EWCA Civ 78 which we commend and on which we give notice we will rely in respect of costs.

Yours faithfully,

....

(Qualifications etc)   Mediator

(Address 1)
(Address 2)
(Telephones)
(E-Mails)

SAMPLE MODEL MEDIATION AGREEMENT

This Mediation Agreement (the "Agreement") is made on [*Insert Date*]

Between

(1) (Name)
   (Address)
   (Telephone)
   (Email)
   Represented by:
   (Legal Advisers details)

And

(2) (Name)
   (Address)
   (Telephone)
   (Email)
   Represented by:
   (Legal Advisers details)

(collectively referred to as "the Parties" and individually as a "Party")

And

(3) .... ("the Mediator")
of the address set out at the head of this document.

WHEREAS

A. A dispute ("the Dispute") has arisen between the Parties, and

B   The Parties have requested the Mediator to assist them to resolve the Dispute by mediation (the "Mediation") in accordance with the terms of the Agreement.

IN CONSIDERATION

of the mutual agreements set out below

IT IS AGREED BETWEEN THE PARTIES AS FOLLOWS:

1. THE MEDIATOR, MEDIATION DATES, VENUE, AND METHOD

1.1 The Parties appoint the Mediator to assist them to resolve the Dispute in accordance with the Agreement.

1.2 If the date or dates and venue of the Mediation are not agreed, they shall be determined in writing by the Mediator after consultation with the Parties.

1.3 If the Parties are unable to reach a settlement during the Mediation, the mediator shall not make any recommendation on possible processes or terms of settlement.

1.4 The Mediator will attempt to effect a resolution by facilitative mediation and The Parties agree that the Mediator may use such skills as reality testing, probing questions, and objective criteria (amongst others) to assist them reach settlement.

1.5 The Parties agree that there shall be deemed to be no binding agreement or binding resolution to the dispute unless a Settlement Agreement is made in writing and signed by The Parties (but not The Mediator). The Settlement Agreement may take such written form as The Parties agree, determine, and wish, including potentially but not limited to, a draft Order, contract, undertaking, or other document.

1.6 The Parties may, if they wish, otherwise conclude heads of agreement, or a minute of matters agreed without making the same binding Settlement Agreement, or they may reach any other form of non-binding resolution. Any offer made in mediation which is intended to survive the mediation should be in writing and so expressed.

2. MEDIATOR NOT TO BE CALLED AS A PARTY OR WITNESS, OR TO BE SUED

2.1 It is an express and fundamental condition precedent of The Mediator agreeing to act that The Parties (whether jointly or severally) shall neither call nor attempt to call The Mediator as a witness in any subsequent matter, or seek a witness statement from him/her, unless an Order to that effect has been obtained by the Court.

2.2 If notwithstanding the foregoing, or in the alternative where an Order so permits, The Parties (jointly or severally) call or attempt to call the Mediator as a witness, or seek a witness statement from him/her, The Parties shall (jointly or severally) be liable to pay The Mediator for The Mediator's recorded time in respect of dealing with or attending upon the summons and/or witness statement at the rate of £250 per hour (plus VAT where applicable) including travel, subsistence, accommodation, and waiting time together with any such legal costs as The Mediator may incur. The Mediator's fees and costs in this instance shall be paid by way of a deposit of £1,000 before any work is undertaken followed by payment of any balance to reach the Mediator within 7 days of each presentation of the Mediator's fee note.

2.3 The Parties also agree that they shall take no action against or commence any action or claim whatsoever against The Mediator arising from this Agreement by reason of his/her acting as The Mediator and that this is also a fundamental condition precedent of The Mediator agreeing to act in this matter. The Parties understand that this precludes any Party seeking any remedy for any alleged negligence or breach of duty or breach of any term of this Agreement by the Mediator.

3. CONFIDENTIALITY AND PRIVILEGE

3.1 As a pre-condition to attendance of any person at the Mediation, that person must sign the Confidentiality Agreement set out at the end of this Agreement.

3.2 Those signing the Confidentiality Agreement and The Parties agree as a condition precedent for their participation in the mediation that the mediation will be conducted on a without prejudice basis and as a private and confidential meeting. Save as set out in paragraph 3.4, nothing said or done or written at or in the Mediation by way of or in the course of discussion, negotiation, exchange of documents, conversation, etc can be repeated or relied upon elsewhere except for the Settlement Agreement.

3.3 During the Mediation itself, The Mediator will not disclose to anyone any statement said to him/her in private without the consent of the person who made that statement, and shall never disclose that statement to any person after the Mediation.

3.4 Provisions (3.2) and (3.3) cannot be varied except by Order of the Court.

3.5 Following termination of the Mediation, all information (whether given orally, in writing or otherwise) produced for, or arising out of or in connection with, the Mediation passing between any of the Parties and/or between any of them and the Mediator and made for the purposes of the Mediation shall be and remain confidential other than as set out in the Settlement Agreement and any terms thereof.

3.6 The Mediator shall not retain any documents or electronic records made or obtained for the purposes of the Mediation other than the signed copy of this Agreement. T h e Mediator will destroy or delete all materials sent to him at the conclusion of the mediation including any notes taken other than the signed copy of this Agreement.

4. START DATE, TIME, AND TERMINATION OF THE MEDIATION

4.1 The Mediation shall begin as follows:

(1)	Date
(2)	Time
(3)	Location
(4)	Duration

4.2 If the duration is exceeded, overtime is payable at the rate of £250 per hour.

Termination

4.3 The Mediation shall terminate either on settlement being reached, or on The Parties agreeing to end the Mediation, or on the duration being reached and no overtime being agreed by The Parties.

4.4 The Mediation may also be terminated by The Mediator when in his/her absolute discretion, which shall not be challenged and for which no reason shall be sought or provided by him/her, The Mediator considers it appropriate to terminate.

5. FEES AND PAYMENT

5.1 Each Party shall pay their agreed share (usually 50% in default of any differing agreement) of The Mediator's fees and expenses which (in total) will be:

(1)	Basic Fee	£
(2)	Overtime	£ 250 per hour (if required by The Parties)
(3)	Travel/expenses	£

5.2 The Mediator's basic fee (plus VAT if appropriate) must be paid before the Mediation begins either by cheque or cleared through a bank transfer unless The Mediator agrees otherwise. The Mediator will provide a fee note to trigger payment.

Cancellation or postponement

5.3 If the Mediation is cancelled or postponed 7 calendar days before the agreed date in paragraph 4.1 above, The Mediator is entitled to 50% of the Basic Fee in paragraph 5.1(1) above. If the mediation is cancelled more than 7 calendar days before the agreed date in paragraph 4.1 above, The Mediator will waive his basic fee but may recover any actual reasonable out of pocket expenses already made (for example travel expenses which are not recoverable).

Adjournment

5.4 If The Parties so agree the Mediation may be adjourned instead of being terminated under paragraph 4.3 above. In such event The Mediator may in his/her discretion agree with The Parties the terms of such an adjournment which will usually be for a fresh mediation fee (if his services are required) based on paragraph 5.1(1) above.

6. APPLICABLE LAW AND DISPUTES

6.1 This Agreement shall be governed by the law of England & Wales.

6.2 The Agreement shall be interpreted to give force to the mediation principles of confidentiality.

IN WITNESS WHEREOF,

The Parties and The Mediator have caused this Agreement to be executed by their undersigned duly authorised representatives

For: _____ By:

[Insert name of Party]

…………………………………….. Dated:

Signature

For: _____ By:

[Insert name of Party]

…………………………………….. Dated:

Signature

For: _____ By:

[Insert name of Mediator]

…………………………………….. Dated:

Signature

MEDIATION ATTENDANCE – CONFIDENTIALITY AGREEMENT

[Note: to be signed by all those in attendance, including The Parties, the Parties' representatives, their lawyers, experts, and any additional advisors to the Parties, any other agreed attendees, and any observers.]

In consideration of my being permitted to attend the Mediation taking place under the provisions of the Agreement to which this is a part, I agree to be personally bound by the Agreement. My attention is specifically drawn to, and I agree personally to be bound by, and/or to bind those or that which I am the authorised representative, Paragraphs 2.1, 2.2, and 2.3 of this Agreement (Exclusion of Liability) and Paragraphs 3.2 and 3.3 (Confidentiality). I will hold confidential all I see or hear at the Mediation subject to the Order of the Court.

Name	Of/ Firm	Role at Mediation	Signature

Draft model mediation email

NB: This is a sample email used for training purposes: the addressees and subject matter are of course fictitious and if there really are such addresses then the reference is accidental. The principles behind the email are, however, sound and potentially useful wherever mediation is used. Mediators are invited to draw ideas from the draft as they wish.

From: dingle@nationalmediation.com
To: lambert@doomedlaw.com; clarke@topdogslaw.com
Subject: Mediation – 1st May 2014 at 1000 at 218 Strand, London

Dear Mr Lambert and Mr Clarke,

Mediation – Villa "Going Down" Ltd v Fortress Hawthorns Ltd

Thank you for your kind instructions to be the mediator in a matter which I understand from the signed Mediation Agreement will be held on 1st May 2013 at 1000. I will be available there from 0900 and note that six hours have been set aside at 218 Strand Mediation Centre, where I know there are plenty of rooms available for you and your respective clients.

    This email is by way of a general introduction. Forgive me if you are familiar with what it says. Please feel free to share it with your clients if you wish.

Conflict check

I do not know any of the participants in the dispute. I am familiar in a general sense with both companies, of course, as they are household names but I do not believe I am conflicted in any way.

My role

My role as a mediator is to use my skills and experience to facilitate resolution. I do not decide anything but will listen carefully to everything that is said and use the information to assist your clients in building a solution with which they are comfortable. I will not provide legal advice. I will ensure that there is a suitable atmosphere for resolution which as you will know is the welcome outcome in more than 90% of mediations.

The process of mediation

Can I suggest that if you or your clients have not mediated before they download and read the useful guide provided at (hyperlink). If there are any questions arising I would be glad to answer them now, or on the day. I will not discuss the merits of the case before the day but can happily explain process, procedure, or resolve administrative matters.

Confidential notes to me before the mediation

I am happy to receive confidential communications setting out (in as much detail as you wish) how you think a settlement might look. I will acknowledge receipt of any such documents to you both but I will not bring them to the mediation but will shred it once I have read it. I am happy to receive information on the day at the mediation if you prefer.

Open documents

Please feel free to send me open documents you think will help me understand what it is you want to achieve. These can be agreed or sent individually. There is no need to prepare anything as formal as a "trial docket". Sometimes a summary of key dates or events is useful, but it is up to you whether you wish to exchange skeleton arguments, chronologies and the like.

Costs

Sometimes people like to come prepared to discuss costs if they are relevant. I stand ready to assist if you think this is appropriate.

Those attending

It would be helpful if you could both let me know before the mediation who is attending – and whether there are any special needs in respect of access or refreshment. I appreciate there may need to be last minute changes which is no problem. You will know that everyone who attends will need to sign the confidentiality clause attached to the mediation agreement.

Observer

As part of mediation training, mediators who have a passed a course are encouraged to observe a minimum of three mediations. Rather like medical students in hospital, they do so confidentially, signing a non-disclosure undertaking, and simply watch and learn. It would be appreciated if you would permit observers but the decision is yours.

<u>Conclusion</u>

I hope that this is a useful introduction: I look forward to seeing you in a few weeks' time.

Kind regards,

Jonathan

Hyperlink example

http://www.clerksroom.com/downloads/281-9476-ClerksRoom-Mediation-Brochure.pdf

Appendix 3: CMC Accredited Mediation Providers 2013/14

Acknowledgement and caveat

The work of CMC Registrar Tracey Stewart (registrar@civilmediation.org) in producing this list is acknowledged: it varies from time to time and it is strongly recommended that potential users check the CMC website regularly. It was correct at the time of writing, 31st December 2013.

Notes

For the Scheme rules and criteria the organisations must meet in order to be Accredited by the Civil Mediation Council, please see the Scheme details in the 'Reference' section of the CMC website at www.civilmediation.org

The CMC accreditation scheme in summary

The scheme applies to organisations, bodies, groups, societies, centres and the like, collectively described as providers. It does not apply to individuals. There is currently no CMC scheme to accredit or certify individual mediators. That is left to provider organisations or to bodies such as the National Mediator Database, the Bar Council, the Law Society, and groups such as the Professional Mediators Association and (it is understood for 2013) the Society of Mediators.

It follows that the provider will continue to carry the responsibility of ensuring that the individual mediator is appropriately trained, insured, supervised and allocated, and fulfils the (Continuing Practice Development (CPD) and practice requirements.

Although there are no restrictions on applications, users should be aware that one of the reasons for originally setting up the scheme was to meet the requirements of the National Mediation Helpline, which was run as part of the Ministry of Justice's commitment to proportionate dispute resolution until funding was lost in 2011.

The CMC scheme is now relied on as a requirement for inclusion in the Directgov "Find a Civil Mediation Provider" database. It is largely self-policing but there is a requirement for a senior official of each candidate provider to sign and date a Statement of Truth personally, certifying that the contents of the application form are true and accurate, upon which the CMC may rely.

The characteristics of an Accredited Provider

The characteristics to be examined by the CMC in the scheme when assessing a candidate provider are broadly:

(a) **Adequate mediator training** – the method by which the candidate has and will continue to admit mediators to membership of its panel, list or group: this includes the minimum training requirement it sets for candidate members, the means by which it assesses whether that training is sufficient and whether the candidate has a sufficient understanding of role and duties of a mediator to be appropriate for admission. The CMC has based its criteria on practice within the civil mediation community in the UK and abroad, but it will refine and may revise its requirements in due course.

(b) **Code of Conduct** – whether the provider has instituted or adopted, and implements, an appropriate Code of Conduct for its members to follow: the CMC endorsed and adopted the EU Model Code of Conduct for Mediators in 2004 and expects that this Code, or a Code of equivalent rigour, should be embraced by an accredited mediation provider.

(c) **Complaints Handling and Feedback** – whether the provider has a published complaints procedure and requires written records to be kept of all complaints.

(d) **Supervision and Mentoring** – the means by which the provider provides adequate and appropriate supervision, mentoring, monitoring and observerships for its mediators; the provider's mediation-specific continuing professional development (CPD) policy and programme or requirements; the scheme the provider adopts for handling comments and feedback; and the opportunity for peer review.

(e) **Insurance** – whether the provider can demonstrate that it has adequate insurance in place for the activities it and its members undertake. Officers and directors insurance is required in addition to mediator insurance where the officers and directors are not panel mediators.

(f) **Efficient administration** – whether the provider can demonstrate that it has suitable and sufficient administrative arrangements that are proportionate to and for the work and workload it undertakes, including the handling of enquiries, the recording of calls, the accurate accounting for fees and the proper rendering of bills to the consumer.

(g) **Allocation of mediators** – the method by which the provider can demonstrate that it ensures (save where the parties decide their own choice of mediator) that an appropriately trained, experienced and skilled mediator is allocated to each case with which it deals.

The specific requirements

The CMC will specifically look for the following important criteria and these are reproduced here to demonstrate the breadth of the scheme, to assist users in deciding whether accreditation is important to them, and to allow those wishing to establish a provider organisation a convenient reference point.

In order to be accredited a provider must meet the following minimum requirements:

A. <u>Size of Panel</u>

An Accredited Mediation Provider must have at least six trained civil or commercial mediators on its panel. You will be asked to provide the names of all panel members as at the date of application or provide a link to such a list.
A mediator on maternity leave or on long term sick leave (which does not exceed 18 months in duration) will continue to count.

B. <u>Mediator Training</u>

(1) An Accredited Mediation Provider's mediators must have successfully completed an assessed training course.

(2) That course must include training in ethics, mediation theory, mediation practice, negotiation, and role play exercises.

(3) If the mediator is not professionally qualified in a discipline which includes law, the mediator must demonstrate a grasp of basic contract law if he/she is to undertake civil or commercial mediations.

(4) For mediators who will have attended a training course up to 31st March 2011, the course and its assessment must have complied with the following requirements:

(i) Performance during or on completion of training must be assessed.

(ii) The training course will include not less than 24 hours of tuition and role-play followed by a formal assessment.

(5) For mediators who attend a training course from 1st April 2011 onwards, the course and its assessment must comply with the following requirements:

(i) Assessors are to meet the criteria of the CMC Accreditation Scheme in terms of training, observations, CPD and practice requirements. Assessors are to be separate from those delivering the training.

(ii) Performance during or on completion of training must contain at least one separate assessment phase of at least one hour where the assessment is continual, and at least two separate assessments of at least one hour each where the assessment is carried out on separate days.

(iii) Assessment criteria are as a minimum to include:–

a) an appropriate and safe environment is set by the participant-mediator which is conductive to problem-solving;

b) the role of mediator to be fully and properly articulated;

c) the principles of confidentiality, neutrality and facilitation be evidenced;

d) trust and rapport be established;

e) necessary skills to explore issues, interests and options be applied;

f) the ability to manage the parties and the process be clear;

g) the ability to advance resolution through the application of negotiation and communication skills be seen;

h) proper consideration of ethical issues as they arise.

(iv)The training course will include not less than 40 hours of face to face tuition and role-play followed by a formal assessment.

Lunch and coffee breaks are excluded.

(v) The training course will include not less than 50% role plays with 50% of these supervised.

(vi) The classroom/lecture setting should not exceed 40 delegates.

(6) An Accredited Mediation Provider bears the responsibility of being satisfied that members have in fact successfully completed a recognised mediation training course and assessment.

The CMC maintains a list of recognised mediation training providers and it is reproduced at Appendix 7.

C. Code of Conduct

(1) An Accredited Mediation Provider must have an appropriate written Code of Conduct for its members to follow.

(2) That written code must be no less rigorous than the EU Model Code of Conduct for Mediators published in 2004.

D. Complaints Handling and Feedback

(1) An Accredited Mediation Provider must have in place a published complaints handling procedure and keep written records of any complaints. All complaints should be followed up and the outcome notified to the complainant within a specified timescale.
(2) An Accredited Mediation Provider must have a feedback system under which it invites, receives, assesses and reviews, both internally and with the mediator, all comments by the parties and their lawyers in respect of mediations.

E. Supervision and Mentoring

(1) An Accredited Mediation Provider must require its new mediators to have observed at least three civil or commercial mediations over the last 12 months before they are eligible for appointment as a lead mediator. One of these observerships may be of a role-play nature.

(2) All the Provider's mediators must have observed or conducted at least two civil or commercial mediations in the 12 months prior to its accreditation (or re-accreditation) in order to ensure that they have current practice experience. This mediation practice requirement can be met by substituting two simulated mediation practice sessions of at least 1 hour each, or one community mediation, or two telephone mediations for one of the two actual or observed mediations that are required.

Where a panel mediator is on maternity leave or long term sickness absence, this period may be extended to 18 months.

(3) The Provider should offer the opportunity for mediators to consult experienced mediators before, during or after each mediation to discuss any issues on which they would benefit from advice.

(4) The Provider should require panel members to undertake at least six hours of mediation-specific CPD per annum in addition to the practice requirements set out above.

These hours may include:

    a) courses offering practical role plays;
    b) attendance at seminars, conferences, tutorials and debates on mediation;
    c) writing articles on mediation;
    d) presenting mediation training, seminars or similar events.

F. Insurance

(1) An Accredited Mediation Provider must have in place insurance cover of not less than £1,000,000 to insure itself against claims that it has negligently administered a mediation.

(2) An Accredited Mediation Provider must either provide or require mediators to obtain and provide evidence of professional liability insurance cover of not less than £1,000,000. Where mediators are doing work involving sums exceeding this amount, an Accredited Mediation Provider must have appropriate insurance cover in place and be able to provide evidence of the same.

G. Efficient administration

An Accredited Mediation Provider should have suitable and sufficient administrative arrangements that are proportionate to and for the work and workload it undertakes, including the handling of enquiries, the recording of calls, the accurate accounting for fees and the proper rendering of bills to the consumer.

H. Allocation of mediators

An Accredited Mediation Provider should have a system of allocating mediations that ensures that an appropriately trained, experienced and skilled mediator is allocated to each case with which it deals.

Organisation (alphabetical order)	**Link to the Organisation website**
Academy of Experts 3 Gray's Inn Square London WC1R 5AH Tel: 020 7430 0333	http://www.academy-experts.org/
ADR Group Grove House Grove Road Redland Briston BS6 6UN Tel: 0117 946 7180	http://www.adrgroup.co.uk/
Association of Cambridge Mediators Sheraton House Castle Park Cambridge CB3 0AX Tel: 01223 370063	http://www.cambridgemediators.co.uk/

Association of Midlands Mediators P O Box 14188 Birmingham B2 2HJ Tel: 0800 633 5460	http://www.midlandsmediators.co.uk/
Association of Northern Mediators ICON Business Centre 4100 Park Approach Thorpe Park Leeds LS15 8GB Tel: 0113 397 0826	http://www.northernmediators.co.uk/
Association of South West Mediators Milsted Langdon Winchester House Dean Gate Avenue Taunton TA1 2UH Tel: 01823 445566	http://www.aswm.org.uk/
Berkeley Square Mediation Ltd Newlands Way Shere Road West Clandon GU4 8SF Tel: 07730 982140	http://berkeleysquaremediation.com/
BL Resolve Blake Lapthorne New Kings Court Tollgate Chandler's Ford Eastleigh Hampshire SO53 3LG Tel: 023 8090 8090	http://www.bllaw.co.uk/services_for_ businesses/mediation.aspx
Canterbury Christ Church University North Holmes Road Canterbury Kent CT1 1QU Tel: 01227 863026	http://www.canterbury.ac.uk/social- applied-sciences/crime-and-policing/ mediation-clinic/Home.aspx

CEDR Solve International Dispute Resolution Centre 70 Fleet Street London EC4Y 1EU Tel: 020 7536 6000	http://www.cedr.com/solve/
Centre for Peaceful Solutions 96 Tubbs Road London NW10 4SB Tel: 020 8453 0086	http://www.centreforpeacefulsolutions.org/
Commercial & Medical Dispute Solutions LLP (CMDS) The Base Dartford Business Park Victoria Road Dartford Kent DA1 5FS Tel: 01322 314820	http://www.cmds.org.uk/
Clerksroom Equity House Blackbrook Park Avenue Taunton Somerset TA1 2RA Tel: 0845 083 3000	http://www.clerksroom.com/mediators.php
Devon & Somerset Law Society (DASLS) Aston Court Pynes Hill Exeter EX2 5AZ Tel: 01392 366333	http://www.dasls.com/uploads/Mediation. pdf?section=1&item=0&pagetitle=Mediati on%20Services
Dispute Mediation Consultancy (DMC) LLP 113b High Street Cowes Isle of Wight PO31 7AX Tel: 07540 333340	http://www.dispute-mediation.co.uk/

Effective Dispute Solutions Ltd (EDSL) 41 Hanover Road Birmingham B65 9EB Tel: 0121 533 2793	http://www.effectivedisputesolutions.co.uk/
Eternal Alliances 3 More London Riverside London SE1 2RE Tel: 020 3283 4260	http://www.eternalalliances.com/
FCMS (Field Court Mediation Service) Field Court Chambers 5 Field Court Gray's Inn London WC1R 5EF Tel: 020 7405 6114	http://www.fieldcourt.co.uk/mediation.htm
Focus Commercial Mediation Ashton House 417 Silbury Boulevard Milton Keynes MK9 2AH Tel: 01908 231132	http://www.focus-mediation.co.uk/
Garden Court Mediation Garden Court Chambers 57 – 60 Lincolns Inn Fields London WC2A 3LJ Tel: 020 7993 7666	http://www.gardencourtmediation.co.uk/
Greater London and East Anglia Mediation LLP St Martin's House 63 West Stockwell Street Colchester Essex CO1 1HE Tel: 01206 217133	http://www.gleamed.co.uk/

Global Mediation Ltd Elwood House 42 Lytton Road Barnet Herts EN5 5BY Tel: 020 8441 1355	http://www.globalmediation.co.uk/
Globis Mediation Group 1 Wheatstone Court Waterwells Business Park Quedgeley Gloucester GL2 2AQ Tel: 0330 100 0809	http://www.globis.co.uk/
Grays Mediation Services LLP Richmond Station Station Yard Richmond DL10 4LD Tel: 0844 264 1880	www.graysmediationservices.co.uk
IDRS Ltd International Dispute Resolution Centre 70 Fleet Street London EC4Y 1EU Tel: 020 7520 3800	http://www.idrs.ltd.uk/
InterMediation International House 1 St. Katherine's Way London E1W 1UN Tel: 020 7977 0600	http://www.inter-resolve.com/home/ mediation/why-mediation
KIDS London SEN Mediation Service 49 Mecklenburgh Square London WC1N 2NY Tel: 020 7837 2900	http://www.kids.org.uk/ information/100885/100924/mediation/

Landmark Chambers 180 Fleet Street London EC4A 2HG Tel: 020 7430 1221	http://www.landmarkchambers.co.uk/mediation
LawWorks Mediation National Pro Bono 48 Chancery Lane London WC2A 1JF Tel: 020 7092 3940	http://www.lawworks.org.uk/
Lyons Davidson Limited Solicitors Victoria House 51 Victoria Street Bristol BS1 6AD Tel: 0117 904 7691	http://www.lddr.co.uk/
Mediation-1st 73 The Close Norwich Norfolk NR1 4DD Tel: 01603 281128	http://www.mediation-1st.co.uk/
Mediation Cumbria 6 Victoria Place Carlisle Cumbria CA1 1ES Tel: 0845 052 3667	http://mediationcumbria.com/
Mediation Solve 20 High Beech Lane Chepstow Monmouthshire NP16 5BQ Tel: 020 7993 6869	http://www.mediationsolve.co.uk/

Middlesex & Thames Valley Mediators 7 Lambscroft Way Chalfont St Peter Buckinghamshire SL9 9AY Tel: 01753 888023	http://www.mtvm.org/
National Mediation Fourth Floor 218 Strand London WC2R 1AT Tel: 0207 353 3936	http://www.nationalmediation.org/
Northern Dispute Resolutions Ltd c/o JK Property Consultants LLP Rotterdam House 116 Quayside Newcastle upon Tyne NE1 3DY Tel: 0191 406 0038	http://www.northerndisputeresolution.co.uk/
North West Mediation Solutions 29 West Leigh Road Blackburn Lancashire BB1 8JR Tel: 01254 720278	http://www.nwmediationsolutions.co.uk/
Oxford Mediation c/o 3 PB 23 Beaumont Street Oxford OX1 2NP Tel: 01865 793736	http://oxford-mediation.com/
Rapproche Civil and Commercial Mediation Purdy House Wickmere Norwich NR11 7LU Tel: 01263 768607	http://www.rapproche.co.uk/services/dispute-mediation/

Royal Institution of Chartered Surveyors Surveyor Court Westwood Way Coventry CV4 8JE Tel: 020 334 3806	http://www.rics.org/drs
Solent & Wessex Civil Mediation Biscoes Solicitors Boyces Cottage The Square Wickham Hampshire PO17 5JN Tel: 01329 833249	http://www.solentmediation.com/
Southern Mediators Sawyers Green Lane Jevington East Sussex BN26 5QD Tel: 01273 311221	http://www.southernmediators.co.uk/
Specialist Mediators LLP Forest Hollow Nursery Lane Nutley East Sussex TN22 3NP Tel: 0845 868 8912	http://www.specialistmediators.org/
Talk Mediation Ltd 41 Bridge Street Hereford HR4 9DG Tel: 01432 344666	http://www.talkmediation.co.uk/
UK Mediation Ltd 8 Green Lane Belper Derbyshire DE56 1BY Tel: 01773 829982	http://www.ukmediation.net/

Wandsworth Mediation Service St Marks Durie Hall Battersea Rise London SW11 1EJ Tel: 020 7223 7744	http://www.wandsworthmediation.co.uk/

Appendix 4: CMC Registered Workplace Mediation Providers

The Civil Mediation Council (CMC) offers a scheme to register workplace provider organisations.

This Appendix extracts material from www.cmcregistered.org and it was felicitous that the former Honorary Secretary of the CMC was Clive Lewis OBE, a leading workplace mediator at *Globis*.

Background

Following the 2007 Gibbons Review, action was taken by the Government to repeal the 2004 Statutory Grievance and Discipline process from 6 April 2009. Employers will now be encouraged to pursue early resolution of workplace disputes, thereby avoiding recourse to employment tribunals.

At their AGM on 10th December 2008 CMC members authorised the CMC Board to develop and introduce the Scheme. The CMC Board approved this Scheme on 12th February 2009 and it went live in April 2009 to support the statutory changes.

The Scheme

The CMC workplace mediation provider registration scheme is the main access channel for users of workplace related mediation services in Great Britain. Those looking for a reputable mediation services provider, are invited find one through this website. The mediation provider will be able to answer any questions you have about the provision of mediation services.

The essence of the Scheme is that it is voluntary but ACAS and other organisations concerned with workplace matters will be encouraged to use, and to recommend that others use, a CMC Registered Workplace Mediation Organisation. It will, however, remain entirely a matter for the users to choose which mediation organisation should be engaged.

For the purposes of this scheme the expression *mediation services in the workplace* means mediations of employment related disputes. Employment related disputes fall into two main categories: workplace mediations deal with disputes where the individual(s) is still an employee of the organization at the commencement of the mediation although a workplace mediation may conclude with a settlement which involves the employee leaving the organisation; employment mediations deal with disputes where the individual(s) is no longer an employee of the organization at the commencement of the mediation, for whatever reason. Mediation organisations encouraged to join the Scheme will be those providing mediation services in any type of workplace dispute in, from, or into England and Wales. Mediation organisations providing such services in, from, or into Scotland are encouraged to join the Scottish Mediation Network and Register (SMN and SMR). There will be clear signposting and links between the CMC and SMR websites.

Those operating wholly abroad may also register should they wish.

Definition of a Workplace Mediator

For the purposes of this Scheme only a Workplace Mediator is defined as a person who has successfully completed the training and assessment process required by the Registered Workplace Mediation Organisation, who has completed at least two full observerships, who is insured and who has complied with the CPD requirements of the Registered Workplace Mediation Organisation. "Workplace Mediator" and "Workplace Mediators" shall are terms used by the CMC according to that definition.

The List

This list was correct as 27th October 2013 but may now be out of date. It should be checked online. The list appears on the CMC website www.cmcregistered.org and has active hyperlinks, information, and contact details.

ACAS

ADR Group

Alliance Mediation Management Ltd

Angel Productions Ltd

Association of Cambridge Mediators

ATOS Healthcare

CEDR

Centre for Peaceful Solutions

Civitas Dispute Resolution

CMP Resolutions

Conflict Resolution Centre

Consensio

Consensus

Eternal Alliances

Focus Mediation

Geoff Lawday Associates

GLEAMED

Global Mediation

Globis

InterMediation

JIB Mediation Services

Lamb Building Mediation Group

Lorraine Bramwell Associates

Lyons Davidson Dispute Resolution

McCormick & Wood Ltd

Mediation at Work

Mediation Works

MTVM

Oxford Mediation

Paradigm Campbell Associates

People Resolutions Ltd

Personal Performance Consultants UK Limited

Solent and Wessex Civil Mediation

Steve Hindmarsh Ltd

Talk Mediation

TCM

UK Mediation Limited

Unite Ltd

Appendix 5: European Code of Conduct for Mediators

Background

The European Union has long recognised the value of mediation in bringing about resolution of disputes and improved access to justice. *It is the Commission view that encouraging the use of mediation and other forms of ADR assists in the resolution of disputes and helps to avoid the worry, time and cost associated with court-based litigation and so assists citizens in a real way to secure their legal rights."*[57]

Following this keen interest and with the assistance of the European Commission, a group of stakeholders developed a European Code of Conduct for Mediators, which was launched at a conference in Brussels on 2 July 2004. The Code sets out a number of principles to which individual mediators can voluntarily decide to commit, under their own responsibility. It is intended to be applicable to all kinds of mediation in civil and commercial matters. Organisations providing mediation services can also make such a commitment, by asking mediators acting under the auspices of their organisation to respect the code. Organisations have the opportunity to make available information on the measures they are taking to support the respect of the code by individual mediators through, for example, training, evaluation and monitoring. The Civil Mediation Council has made it a requirement of accreditation that provider organisations adhere to the Code or to some similar code.

For the purposes of the code mediation is defined as any process where two or more parties agree to the appointment of a third-party – "the mediator" – to help the parties to solve a dispute by reaching an agreement without adjudication and regardless of how that process may be called or commonly referred to in each Member State. While enjoying the support of the European Commission, the Code is not intended to represent its official position. Instead, it can be seen as being the Justice Directorate's way of supporting a self-regulatory approach to ADR by the ADR community. Adherence to the code is stated to be without prejudice to national legislation or rules regulating individual professions.

[57] http://ec.europa.eu/civiljustice/adr/adr_ec_en.htm

EUROPEAN CODE OF CONDUCT FOR MEDIATORS

4th June 2004

1. COMPETENCE AND APPOINTMENT OF MEDIATORS

1.1 Competence

Mediators shall be competent and knowledgeable in the process of mediation. Relevant factors shall include proper training and continuous updating of their education and practice in mediation skills, having regard to any relevant standards or accreditation schemes.

1.2 Appointment

The mediator will confer with the parties regarding suitable dates on which the mediation may take place. The mediator shall satisfy him/herself as to his/her background and competence to conduct the mediation before accepting the appointment and, upon request, disclose information concerning his/her background and experience to the parties.

1.3 Advertising/promotion of the mediator's services

Mediators may promote their practice, in a professional, truthful, and dignified way.

2. INDEPENDENCE AND IMPARTIALITY

2.1 Independence and neutrality

The mediator must not act, or, having started to do so, continue to act, before having disclosed any circumstances that may, or may be seen to, affect his or her independence or conflict of interests. The duty to disclose is a continuing obligation throughout the process. Such circumstances shall include

- any personal or business relationship with one of the parties,
- any financial or other interest, direct or indirect, in the outcome of the mediation, or
- the mediator, or a member of his or her firm, having acted in any capacity other than mediator for one of the parties.

In such cases the mediator may only accept or continue the mediation provided that he/she is certain of being able to carry out the mediation with full independence and neutrality in order to guarantee full impartiality and that the parties explicitly consent.

2.2 Impartiality

The mediator shall at all times act, and endeavour to be seen to act, with impartiality towards the parties and be committed to serve all parties equally with respect to the process of mediation.

3. THE MEDIATION AGREEMENT, PROCESS, SETTLEMENT AND FEES

3.1 Procedure

The mediator shall satisfy himself/herself that the parties to the mediation understand the characteristics of the mediation process and the role of the mediator and the parties in it.

The mediator shall in particular ensure that prior to commencement of the mediation the parties have understood and expressly agreed the terms and conditions of the mediation agreement including in particular any applicable provisions relating to obligations of confidentiality on the mediator and on the parties.

The mediation agreement shall, upon request of the parties, be drawn up in writing. The mediator shall conduct the proceedings in an appropriate manner, taking into account the circumstances of the case, including possible power imbalances and the rule of law, any wishes the parties may express and the need for a prompt settlement of the dispute. The parties shall be free to agree with the mediator, by reference to a set of rules or otherwise, on the manner in which the mediation is to be conducted. The mediator, if he/she deems it useful, may hear the parties separately.

3.2 Fairness of the process

The mediator shall ensure that all parties have adequate opportunities to be involved in the process. The mediator if appropriate shall inform the parties, and may terminate the mediation, if:

– a settlement is being reached that for the mediator appears unenforceable or illegal, having regard to the circumstances of the case and the competence of the mediator for making such an assessment, or

– the mediator considers that continuing the mediation is unlikely to result in a settlement.

3.3 The end of the process

The mediator shall take all appropriate measures to ensure that any understanding is reached by all parties through knowing and informed consent, and that all parties understand the terms of the agreement.

The parties may withdraw from the mediation at any time without giving any justification. The mediator may, upon request of the parties and within the limits of his or her competence, inform the parties as to how they may formalise the agreement and as to the possibilities for making the agreement enforceable.

3.4 Fees

Where not already provided, the mediator must always supply the parties with complete information on the mode of remuneration which he intends to apply. He/she shall not accept a mediation before the principles of his/her remuneration have been accepted by all parties concerned.

4. CONFIDENTIALITY

The mediator shall keep confidential all information, arising out of or in connection with the mediation, including the fact that the mediation is to take place or has taken place, unless compelled by law or public policy grounds. Any information disclosed in confidence to mediators by one of the parties shall not be disclosed to the other parties without permission or unless compelled by law.

For more information see the Civil Mediation Council site www.civilmediation.org

Appendix 6: List of Useful Mediation Links

NB: *CMC Mediation Providers are listed at Appendix 2 above*
      CMC Workplace Providers are listed at Appendix 3 above
      CMC Recognised Training Organisations are listed at Appendix 7 below

These highly selective and incomplete links here are divided into five sections:

(1) Government and Judiciary
(2) Civil Mediation Council
(3) Other Professional Bodies
(4) Cases
(5) Other Materials

These links will vary from time to time – in particular those on government sites appear to move with considerable rapidity: please notify the authors of any broken links through their email: handbook@schoolofmediation.org

(1) Government and Judiciary

Ministry of Justice mediation main page
www.justice.gov.uk/courts/mediation

HM Courts and Tribunals Service mediation manual
www.judiciary.gov.uk/resources/jco/documents/guidance/civil_court_mediation_service_manual_v3_mar09.pdf

DirectGov Mediation
www.direct.gov.uk

Court of Appeal Mediation Pilot
http://www.judiciary.gov.uk/media/media-releases/2012/news-release-mediation-pilot-court-of-appeal

(2) Civil Mediation Council

Website for Civil Mediation Council
www.civilmediation.org

Website of CMC Registered Workplace Providers
www.cmcregistered.org

Downloads of dozens of useful documents and speeches
www.civilmediation.org/downloads.php?f=17

POCA & Money Laundering – duties of a mediator
www.civilmediation.org/downloads.php?f=46

(3) Other Professional Bodies

The Society of Mediators pages
www.societyofmediators.org

Law Society mediation pages
www.lawsociety.org.uk/for_the_public/accredited-specialists/civil-commercial-mediation/

Bar Council mediation pages
www.barcouncil.org.uk/about-the-bar/find-a-barrister/mediation-directory/

Family Mediation Council
www.familymediationcouncil.org.uk

College of Mediators (family mediation)
www.collegeofmediators.co.uk

Law Works Pro Bono Mediation
www.lawworks.org.uk

(4) Cases – available on BAILLI

Dyson & Field exors of Lawrence Twohey dec'd -v- Leeds City Council (C of A 22 Nov 1999)

Cowl -v- Plymouth City Council [2001] EWCA Civ 1935

Dunnett -v- Railtrack [2002] EWCA Civ 302

McMillan Williams –v- Range [2004] EWCA Civ 294

Halsey –v- Milton Keynes General NHS Trust [2004] EWCA 3006 Civ 576

Daniels –v- The Commissioner of Police for the Metropolis [2005] EWCA Civ 1312

Burchell NF –v- Mr & Mrs Bullard [2005] EWCA Civ 358

Egan –v- Motor Services (Bath) Ltd [2007] EWCA Civ 1002

Rolf v De Guerin [2011] EWCA Civ 78

(5) Other Materials

London School of Mediation resources
www.schoolofmediation.org

Mediation In Judicial Review
http://www.publiclawproject.org.uk/documents/MJRhandbookFINAL.pdf

Appendix 7: CMC Recognised Mediation Training Organisations

Background

Many organisations purport to offer accredited training to the general public in civil and commercial mediation. The Civil Mediation Council (CMC) has, with the assistance of an academic group, recognised since 2009 the training organisations set out below as meeting the required criteria to train mediators who will be appropriate for membership of an CMC Accredited Mediation Provider.

Some of the organisations are also approved by the Law Society and the Bar Council. Each organisation will provide details in respect of their approval process, standards, and documentation if requested.

The list is correct at 31st October 2012 but reference should be made to the CMC from time to time to ensure that it is up to date.

The List

Academy of Experts — www.academy-experts.org
ADR Chambers (UK) — www.adrchambers.co.uk
ADR Group — www.adrgroup.co.uk
CEDR — www.cedr.com
Chartered Institute of Arbitrators — www.ciarb.org
Core Solutions — www.core-solutions.com
London School of Mediation — www.schoolofmediation.org
MATA — www.mata.org.uk
School of Psychotherapy & Counselling Psychology, Regents College — www.spc.ac.uk

RICS — www.rics.org
UK Mediation — www.ukmediation.net

Appendix 8: Authors' Pocket Biographies

Jonathan Dingle

www.218strand.com

Jonathan is a leading mediator and common law barrister. He was a founder of and Secretary to the Civil Mediation Council for 8 years. Jonathan graduated from King's College London and originally trained in conciliation in Southampton in 1979. Following his call to the Bar by the Middle temple in 1986, he later trained as a commercial mediator with Stitt, Feld & Handy for ADR Chambers in London and attended courses with organisations including JAMS in New York. He is an authority on all matters mediation. Jonathan is a founder and lead tutor of London School of Mediation. He retired from the Royal Navy as a Commander in which he served on operations, in wartime, and later in the Ministry of Defence. He was appointed a Judge Advocate in 1991 and holds a further part-time judicial appointment. A past Legal Chair of Football League Disciplinary Panels, he is regularly asked to speak on mediation around the globe and is an international trainer of repute.

Jonathan@218strand.com   **0207 353 3936**

Judith Kelbie

www.jhkllp.com

Judith trained as a mediator with Stitt, Feld & Handy for ADR Chambers in London and attended courses with organisations including JAMS in New York. She is a senior Solicitor and runs her own litigation practice from North Yorkshire. Elected as an independent board member of the Civil Mediation Council for 6 years, she chaired the Accreditation Committee responsible for standards and the Outreach Committee responsible for organising conferences and forums. Judith is a founder and Director of London School of Mediation of which she is a lead tutor. She is an active international mediator with a reputation for assisting participants to reach a solution in some of the seemingly most intractable cases. Judith speaks on mediation internationally, and has presented papers at mediation conferences and forums in Paris, Warsaw, Vienna, Auckland, Cochin, Dublin, Belfast, and Lisbon. She is also a qualified electronics engineer and was a commissioned officer in the Royal Navy.

judith@jhkllp.com   **01423 87 4567**

London School of Mediation Limited

www.schoolofmediation.org   **0207 427 0848**
courses@schoolofmediation.org

The Old Bull Mediation

(Note: All names, places, companies, and organisation are fictional and bear no relation to the actual participants in a similar mediation. Any perceived passing resemblance to similar names is coincidental and unintended).

It was a wet March weekend. There had been little trade in the restaurant. In fact, for several months now the Old Bull restaurant on the edge of Appleby had been in decline. There was talk in the village of it having to close, despite Jim and Judy's best efforts. So it was with some surprise, and perhaps pleasure, that the locals saw the posters announcing the arrival of fitters to refurbish the sixteenth century building, in early April. Jim and Judy were to be congratulated for raising the funds.

The first smoke was detected around two in the morning. Its pervasive smell reached the nostrils of the ancient Labrador, who barked and was told firmly by Jim to be quiet. The fire alarm activated ten minutes later, by which time the laundry at the back of the building was in full blaze. Judy dialled 999 as Jim sought to fight the blaze with the extinguishers, but only succeeded in letting it spread into the lounge. He opened the safe, took the contents, and his favourite jacket from behind a door, and made sure Judy and the dog were outside.

The village and the fire brigade arrived ten minutes later and the fire was out in thirty minutes. The restaurant was, however, wrecked. That which was not burned was smoke or water damaged. Only the wine cellar, with its heavy door, and the garage with Jim's collection of motorcycles, were unscathed. Neighbours and sympathy were followed by loss adjusters and claims inspectors.

Three Tigers Underwriting, who insured the Old Bull under a new policy written by a broker just six weeks earlier, were not happy with the claim. The fire officers could not trace an obvious electrical fault or a real cause. A melted *Lemon* laptop found where a desk had stood in the tiny reservations area next to the laundry was suggested as the blame. This had been bought from the *LemonStore* in Birmingham just three months earlier.

Lemon denied liability as did *Three Tigers* and in the background there were vague suggestions of arson, never fully articulated. Jim and Judy were outraged: they had both been in the Army and had Long Service medals. They instructed 7 Solicitors LLP to bring a claim against, well anyone who might allow them to live the dream. Letters of claim were despatched and the potential defendants in turn found their panel lawyers willing to repel boarders.

7 Solicitors sought respected experts, as did *Three Tigers* and *Lemon*. There were accountants and witnesses, friends, and disclosure. £560,000 was claimed, rising with every passing week through loss of income. The partner with conduct invited the defendants to mediate with a strong reminder of the costs of not doing so: or the claim would be issued. Both defendants, represented by leading Birmingham firms of solicitors well used to the local judiciary's injunctions to use the courts as a last resort, agreed. Five months after the fire, and just two weeks after the mediation offer, the three groups arrived at *The Hawthorns* close to the M5 where they were shown into separate rooms, all of which had a view of the Premier League turf: but were soundproof, private, and discreet. The mediator welcomed them individually and checked that they had signed the agreement to mediate, that each group had authority, and would be ready to begin at 1030. They had, and would be.

Twenty minutes later, seventeen people met in the Jeff Astle Boardroom, around a large table, amid expectation and looking to the mediator. Jim and Judy had their solicitor and a barrister. *Lemon* appeared through their European general counsel, and with two further solicitors, together with a trainee and a pile of legal pads. *Three Tigers* sent two underwriters, a solicitor, a barrister and a man they described as their investigator and his assistant. The group was completed by the mediator and two observers – on this occasion doctors from the local NHS Trust who had completed a mediation course and were learning to become mediators in addition to their day job.

"Welcome, and thank you for instructing me to be your mediator today. My name is Helen and as your know I am by profession an accountant: and as it happens I am also a keen cook. But neither of these roles is important because I am here to help you resolve the impasse you have reached. We have six hours available and I understand that you are all available for that time: is that right?"

It was and the nods indicated that all present were listening intently to Helen's easy style and comfortable tone. She explained the whereabouts of tea and toilets, fire escapes and internet in the same pleasant manner before turning to detail.

"Thank you to those who prepared all the various documents, plans, and papers: I have read them all and I can understand the work that has gone into them. You can take it as a given I am familiar with the back-story.

"What I shall be asking you to do in a moment, is to tell me in turn what, in general terms, you hope to achieve from today – and I do not mind who starts. You have all had my email introduction to mediation so I need hardly remind you that I do not decide anything or need to be persuaded - you are here to persuade each other. I will not offer legal or financial advice: you have your professionals to do that, but with your permission I will ask questions which may challenge you. It is called reality testing and is to allow me better to understand how you see the settlement options.

"For my part I am confident that there is a settlement to be had today – you will know that more than 90% of mediations so conclude and given that you have told me you are here in good faith and with authority, the signs are good. So if you will give me permission if I think it will help to play Devil's Advocate it will help me to assist you – you know that everything that is said here is confidential and without prejudice, and that you do not have to answer any questions, whether we are working together round this table or in private back in your respective rooms: is that alright?"

In turn all the participants agreed to this sensible arrangement. They went on to agree as well that they could be called by their first names, even the very senior barrister who travelled up from London. Helen made a note of the names and each of the roles and made sure they were visible on a table map in front of her. She thanked everyone for letting the observers complete their training and pointed out that they had signed a confidentiality agreement and had no knowledge of any of the participants.

"Finally, people sometimes tell me that a rule that only one person speaks at once helps them focus on what is being said. Is that a rule you would like to adopt?"

It was, for all, and they could not suggest any other rules except that mobile phones should be on silent and there would be no recording of what was said. The participants also agreed that they knew that Helen would destroy any notes she might make and could not be called as a witness by anyone after the mediation.

"So," said Helen, eight minutes after she had brought everyone together, "with a reminder that I have read the carefully prepared briefs you have sent me outlining the background to the dispute, who would like to begin by telling me what you would like to achieve?"

Max, counsel for Jim and Judy, piped up: "I would like to start, if nobody minds?" No one did. "Helen, you will have seen from the papers that Jim and Judy are both respected citizens, who have invested their savings in the Old Bull. I know that you want to hear what it is they want to achieve from today, but it is also important to understand how they got to being where they are today – and what until that horrible night, what they had achieved."

"They had built a restaurant, a business, a base of clients, and a chance to invest for the future. They were earning, on the previous year's figures, at least £1,000 a week profit. They had a home, a position in the village, and security. Now they have nothing more than a wine-cellar, and a few possessions in rented accommodation with their Labrador.

"What they want to achieve is a recognition of what they had, and where they would have been, but for the fire. They do not care if *Lemon* meets the bill, or *Three Tigers*, or the man in the moon quite frankly – but they want the wherewithal from someone to rebuild, move, on and deal with their losses. That is why my latest schedule outlines £636,000 as the figure to do all of this – with interest but in addition there are the legal costs."

Helen had watched Max, not making notes, and also made eye contact with Jim and Judy. She thanked Max and asked him if she could just clarify a couple of things: of course, said counsel.

"Were either of Jim or Judy injured in the fire?" Both shook their heads. "And the dog that barked in the night?" Judy's eyes opened – it was the first human acknowledgement Helen had seen in her face. "He was fine – we wished we had paid more attention to his woofing. Did you know Jim shouted at him to be quiet, thought the mutt was dreaming of rabbits." The couple smiled at each other. Helen caught a glimpse of heads exchanging looks on the other side of the table. She made a mental note to ask about that in private later – perhaps putting it to the investigator. Helen, though continued.

"Thank you Judy – could you help me with this: are either you or Jim working now. I think I read towards the end of the files you sent me that you are both trained chefs?"

"Can I deal with that a little later," asked Max. Helen assured him that he could and then asked what else he or anyone else would like to say on behalf of Judy or Jim. There was nothing so she looked around the table, to *Lemon's* team. Would they or *Three Tigers* like to go next?

Lemon's general counsel Portia asked to make a statement. It was agreed she could. "I would first of all like to say that all of us, as individuals around the table, can only imagine what it is like to lose not only a home but also a livelihood, however tenuous, to a fire. Speaking for myself can I therefore say how sorry I was, and indeed all I have spoken to at *Lemon* to hear of the fire?

Judy, all military politeness, began to say thank you, though Portia continued.

"But let's be clear at the same time, Helen – *Lemon's* sympathy is wholly without prejudice for we utterly deny that the laptop caused the fire. We reject the attempt to cast the blame upon a company that for the last twenty years has been at the heart of everything that is good and innovative in personal computing.

"We want to use today to point out that our products are safe, that we have no reason to be in any claim and that while, as I say, we all have sympathy with Jim and Judy, there is nothing to be gained by *Lemon* being a party to any action which will be vigorously defended. In a sense *Lemon* would welcome the chance to clear its good name in court but to be frank we do not need the distraction with the launch of the new L-Tab in a few months, and the L-Talk5 being such a successful new Smartphone. Why, I see that even Toby has one!"

Portia smiled at *Three Tiger's* senior underwriter who was clearly engaged in something on his device. It was put down rather sheepishly but a point, though to what effect Helen was not sure, had been made. Using the pause, Helen asked:

"Portia, thank you for identifying your client's ambitions – do you want to tell me a little about the detail of the L-Top that was found in the Old Bull? For example – I am not clear whether it was made in Europe or further afield?"

Portia's smile vanished – insofar as it was relevant, she told Helen, the laptop was wholly made in South Wales using chips from the United States. It was European. She would prefer to deal with any other matters in private. Would any of Portia's team like to add anything? They would not and Portia returned to the fore by saying that "*Lemon* would finally want to make it clear that it does not associate itself with any allegations of arson here. The most likely cause so far as we can see of the fire is some electrical connection that was wholly destroyed in the intensity of the blaze or washed away by hoses. We agree with Jim and Judy that they are the innocent victims here but of course do not accept the figures that Max has contrived so eloquently to put together for the losses – not that *Lemon* has an interest in that."

Helen used the cue – she turned face the group representing *Three Tigers*. Could she ask whether for the purposes of today arson was alleged? It was not. It might be, suggested Freddie, their counsel, if the claim did not resolve, but it was not something that they wished Helen to deal with at mediation.

"Thank you, Freddie – so what do *Three Tigers* want to achieve from today?"

Freddie set out his stall, in a crisp courtroom style slightly at odds with the relative informality of what had gone on already. His instructions were both to challenge the right of Jim and Judy to seek their compensation from *Three Tigers* at all, and to press *Lemon* to recognise its responsibility. Without prejudice he was accompanied by his client's special investigators and he would like them to speak to *Lemon* with Helen being present but not Jim and Judy.

"We also want to make it clear", Freddie continued, "that we do not believe the figures that Max has advanced and see that there is a clear failure to mitigate in respect of other employment on the part of Max's clients. This claim, even were it to stick at my clients' door would not be worth anything like the figure that was being levied in the opening session."

Before Helen could ask a number of questions she was framing, Portia piped up again. She asked Helen if she and her team could have a private meeting with the mediator to discuss what had just been said. It was, Portia suggested, not what they had expected and they wished to deal with some procedural questions. Perhaps they might have five or so minutes?

Helen responded that participants often asked for private sessions with the mediator and anything said in them would be confidential. She would not disclose what was said to her unless she was permitted to do so: the sessions were rather like time spent by a patient with a General Practitioner. She suggested ten minutes and if more time was needed then she would come and seek permission from Max and Freddie. Once she had spoken to Portia, then perhaps a further round table or open meeting might be held, or a series of private meetings. Everyone would have an equal chance to meet her.

The meeting broke up tolerably amicably and Helen joined Portia and the *Lemon* group in their room which was Box 17. William, one of the solicitors for *Lemon* offered the coffee whilst they all sat down. "How can I help?" asked Helen "What was it that you could not say to the meeting as a whole?"

"Well," began Portia, "we are here to settle this but we want to do so privately. Everything we say to you is confidential, right?"

Helen nodded. Portia went on.

"It is remotely possible that the L-Top which seems to have been in the Old Bull had a battery issue. Not likely or even probable. But we have noticed in some very extreme tests that if someone, contrary to the instructions in the online user manual, leaves the L-Top on charge for more than about a month, in other words treats it as a desk top, then we can get issues with the fan that cools the transformer in certain very humid conditions.

"We have never seen an issue in Europe, but in a number of southern states in the USA there have been reported high temperatures. Now I hasten to add that all L-Tops sold in the US since last April have had a minor firmware re-write and there have been no claims or fires. It would seem, though, that Judy's L-Top was a UK model with the original configuration and it is just conceivable, in the moist air near the laundry room, that a similar set of circumstances arose.

"No more than just conceivable and no one must ever know that *Lemon* contributed to a settlement. If we do settle, we want it to appear to be from *Three Tigers*."

"Have you discussed this with Freddie, or anyone at *Three Tigers*?" asked Helen. Portia had not and hoped to use today to do that. "We would like to try the framework of the mediation to make an approach to them: we feel that it would be less awkward."

"Can you tell me why?" asked Helen.

"Well, we do not actually trust them – or more properly their investigation team. We have had, shall we say, issues in the past and do not want what we said to be transmitted beyond the underwriters – and of course Freddie."

"Go on..."

"Look, Dan Purchase, who is their so called expert on forensic fire analysis, was the lead man on a case where it was said a *LemonStore* in Newcastle burned down because of a faulty L-Desk, our PC equivalent. For lots of reasons we could not disclose to them, blackmail and so on, we knew that the store had been maliciously targeted but Purchase gave evidence that it could only have been the L-Desk. We knew that was incorrect."

"So what you are telling me is that you are looking for a commercial settlement with nothing to be disclosed to either Judy or Jim, on the one hand, or Dan and his assistant Jessica on the other?"

Portia confirmed that was right – she had authority to spend up to £200,000 today but no more so things would be tight. Helen was about to ask why that sum - then noticed that the ten minutes were almost up. She asked how Portia she would like this taken forward. "We would like you to be a sort of neutral chair in a meeting between ourselves and the professionals from *Three Tigers*. Could you do that?"

Helen said she would ask – she would need to see both Freddie's team and ask Max for some time to set up a meeting, but would not of course disclose what had been said or the reason. Was that acceptable? It was, and spot on ten minutes Helen left to make the administrative arrangements. Jim and Judy were happy – Max explained to them that these sorts of bipartisan talks were normal, and Freddie was curious but agreeable. Twenty minutes later, Helen was back in Box 17.

"Portia, Freddie – thank you for inviting me to chair this side meeting – Dan and Jessica are back in Box 15 and Max and his group are happy in their room. I said we might need twenty minutes initially, is that OK?" It was, and Helen reminded everyone that this session was off the record, without prejudice and was on the basis that nothing said could be repeated outside the room without everyone's consent. That was agreed. Blue counsels' notebooks were firmly closed on the table. All eyes were on Portia.

"Thank you Helen. Look, Freddie, gentlemen, the truth is that *Lemon* simply does not have time for this malarkey and is not inclined to have the likes of Dan offering up what we consider to be specious evidence. We have a multi-million launch just a few weeks away and this distraction will not do. We see you wholly in the frame but are prepared to soften the blow for you. I will cut straight to the chase. *Lemon* will, under a guarantee that no one is ever aware of the deal, put £50,000 into the settlement pot just to make this go away.

"You should know though that we have real suspicions about this case although we can prove nothing. Like you we do not see this as being worth anything like the sum claimed. Indeed while we cannot argue with the damage to the Old Bull itself, and have to accept the restoration quotes at £300,000, we cannot see the balance including their costs exceeding £200,000. It follows that our contribution is around 10%."

Helen said nothing. She had listened carefully and while Portia had, in their private session referred to a small chance that the L-Top had been to blame she had obviously chosen her words with skill and precision in this session. She had not denied there was a possible fault merely sought to traverse the question. There was, accordingly, Helen assessed no abuse of her neutrality, simply active negotiation. How would Freddie respond?

Freddie was seemingly unphased. He glanced briefly at his team – Mohammed and Peter – and then spoke with apparent easy assurance.

"Portia, we all know there is something up here. We are not sure what but we are pretty sure you know something and *Lemon* would like to buy out of the risk that it will come to light. Let's stop pretending shall we and if you make us a sensible offer we will look at it."

Helen, who thus far had sat a little back in her chair, leaned forward. The eyes switched to her as she moved; perhaps sensing that she was going to head off a potential confrontation.

"Could I just ask, is there a measure of agreement between you on how much the claim might be worth – or to put it another way, how much Jim and Judy might take to settle? Would it be worth exploring that before you consider contributions?" Portia and Freddie looked at each other and agreed that it would not do any harm. It might be useful though to know what the claimants were really after. Would Helen like to go and ask?

"If you were in Max's shoes," Helen asked, "having set out your stall in opening and in the schedule of loss at £636,000, would you immediately bid against yourself at this stage? What would you want, were you Max, to cause you to move?"

Portia and Freddie agreed they would need some leverage and Helen asked what they might be able to offer Max. They thought the focus should be on a failure to find work and a failure to appreciate how long the refurbishment would have dented trade in any event even if there had been to fire.

Working together, Portia and Freddie with their teams soon came up with a formula that diminished the claim to a little under £400,000. They all thought this was a good opening and invited Helen to take it through to the third room and discuss it with Judy and Jim. "Please make sure that it is not conveyed as an offer, but simply as a how we are looking at the theoretical value of the case."

Having tested a number of the assumptions underpinning their arguments, to understand why they were advocating the figure, Helen asked them to write this down for clarity. She then suggested that she might leave them together to discuss some of the residual issues while she visited Max and the claimants. She again asked for twenty minutes. Pausing in the long corridor, festooned with football memorabilia, the mediator asked her observers how they thought it was going. Neither doctor seemed confident. Helen smiled to herself and knocked on Judy and Jim's door.

"Max, I have an analysis of the claim value from Freddie and Portia – would you like to see it?" asked Helen, lightly brandishing the paper which bore Freddie's distinctive copper plate handwriting. Max nodded and Helen continued "when you have read it would you honour me with your thoughts as to why they have taken this approach?"

"Three hundred and ninety eight thousand pounds!" exclaimed Max having read the bottom line of the proposal. "That is not even two thirds of the claim. And it is not even an offer – just a suggested calculation of loss. It is well, outrageous!"

Helen noticed that neither Jim not Judy, nor the partner from 7 Solicitors seemed to share the angst that Max was displaying. They were instead looking at the calculations. She decided to ask the same question she had begun with in Box 17.

"Jim, Judy – could I ask, as the lawyers reflect on the analysis, what was important to you that did not come across in the opening meeting we had? As you know, whatever you say here is private and I will not repeat."

It was Judy who replied. "Look, Helen, we just want to move on. Fix up the place, sell it and try our luck in another line of business. To be honest, we cannot really abide the thought of living in a place where there was a fire." Max glanced up from his perusal of the papers. Neither he nor the partner had heard this before. Helen invited her to continue.

"We have been thinking" Jim put in "and in the months in our rented cottage we have had to adapt. It started by chance – we were doing some online menu planning and realised that we both liked designing the menus and food as much as serving it. So we have taught ourselves online publishing, with blogs and so forth – and we intend to write and sell online cookery books.

"The first one is almost done – it is called 'Marching on its Stomach' and is about the very best of armed forces food. We are going to give part of the profit to charity and really use the idea of the military wives choir to sell military wives' cooking."

Helen looked at both the lawyers. The partner was first to react – so what do you need to make this a reality, she asked? How soon did they want to get going?

Judy said they had used the last few months wisely and had everything lined up – a web-designer, a photographer, even someone who could do YouTube links and a whole bunch of past and present military wives. But they needed around £100,000 to take care of the set up costs, their living expenses, and the move – all over the cost of refurbishing the Old Bull.

"Plus your legal fees" put in Max the barrister.

"How much are they?" asked Helen. The partner produced a one page summary. They were £26,400 including VAT and disbursements, plus the one third cost of the mediation, which was £1,200 including hire of the rooms.

"Can I share this with the others?"

"Not yet" said Max, "we don't want them making a global offer and trying to split us from our clients". The partner looked at Helen. She seemed to be rather less belligerent.

"Could you make that a precondition of disclosure, that there were no global offers? I only ask because I wonder if you were looking after the interests of those paying would you want to know your total exposure before agreeing any damages?"

The lawyers agreed they would and that they could do that, but first needed their clients to agree a figure. If what they were really seeking was refurbishment plus £100,000 plus costs, it seemed to the lawyers that a good starting point would be to offer to split the difference – to horse trade at say £520,000 with costs on top.

Helen asked them what reaction that might lead to in the other rooms. They all seemed confident that it would be well received. Having asked Freddie whether he wanted to write it or to put the offer directly across an open table, Helen soon found herself with amendments to the copper plate returning to Box 17 just as twenty minutes were up. She knocked on the door and entered to find only the *Lemon* team present – Portia said that Freddie would like to see her in Box 21. Helen made her way down there without disclosing the offer as it was addressed to both potential payers. Freddie greeted her. Dan and Jessica were absent.

"Can we talk openly," asked Mohammed. Of course.

"Look the reality is we have no evidence that the L-Top caused anything. Did *Lemon* tell you anything – we would really appreciate knowing what is driving their offer?" "What do you think is driving it?" asked Helen, smoothly moving over the invitation to breach the confidentiality of the first private session with Portia. "Did you ask when I was with Jim and Judy?"

"Yes we did – and they simply said 'good business' – now we know that makes no sense." Helen stayed silent and cocked her head. Mohammed continued.

"Look, I suppose it does not matter. We know we are stuffed and we only brought Dan and Jessica along to pretend we knew something. Frankly, we have nothing but smoke and mirrors…" Max groaned at the allusion," …and whatever we can get is a bonus. But – and it is big but – we do not want *Lemon* to know our weakness. How can we do that Helen?"

Helen thought for a moment and turned to Freddie and Graham the solicitor from Marlowes LLP, representing *Three Tigers*. What did they suggest?

The consensus was that there could be a bullish front and a response to any proposal from the claimants could be worked out. *Lemon* could be invited to pay 50% on a risk basis – but anything would be good.

Helen invited them to rejoin the *Lemon* group in Box 17 where she would disclose the offer that Jim and Judy had given her simultaneously to both. A few minutes later she had done so and asked why Freddie or Portia thought that the offer was pitched in the way it was?

"Costs are pretty reasonable compared to some we see – mention no names," interjected Graham, to shared murmurs "but I expect they will come down a little. £25,000 should see them happy". Portia took up the running on the main claim.

"OK," she began "while £520,000 is more rational than £636,000 I think there is room to manoeuvre, still on the basis of mitigation and uncertainty. I think the evidence from their accountant is attackable as best case. I think if we offered £450,000 plus costs that might just make it."

"We?" inquired Helen

"Well I mean *Lemon* accept that they have to make some contribution."

"What would it look like if the settlement were £450,000 plus costs?"

Freddie jumped in, as Portia paused. "We would expect you to take half of the running here. Minimum. Bottom Line. So if they buy it you would be in for £238,000 with both of us bearing our own costs."

"That is not going to happen, Freddie. That would not be good business or risk avoidance. That would be sharing and we both know there is no evidence to justify that approach. The most I can contribute today is £100,000 global. Take it our leave it."

"Can we have a moment in private" asked Freddie – and the *Three Tigers* team withdrew. Helen stayed with Portia and asked simply what *Lemon* would do if the insurers rejected that approach. Portia said they would make their best and final offer: whatever that may be but would need to know first what the claimants would take.

Freddie re-appeared and said that they could accept £100,000 from *Lemon* only if Jim and Judy accepted the offer. If they wanted more, then the balance would have to come from the computer giant.

Helen asked how they wanted to make the offer – bearing in mind *Lemon's* insistence on privacy. Portia suggested that Freddie and his team meet with Max and his group and see if they could thrash out a deal. **Lemon** could therefore appear to be playing no part in the settlement as far as the outside world were concerned.

The bipartite meeting was arranged back in the Boardroom with Helen in the chair.

"Freddie – I believe you have an offer for Jim and Judy?"

Freddie explained that much against their better judgment, **Three Tigers** were now persuaded to go to £450,000 plus costs which they would limit to £25,000 all in. This really was as much as Max could reasonably hope to recover. Max, however, had already taken instructions and, Helen noticed, had managed to brief his clients to keep poker faces.

"Thanks Freddie, had you come back at £480,000 plus costs at £27,500 including today then we would have had some risk. I can assure my clients that there is none at present so we are stuck. Would you like to take instructions?"

Freddie looked at the team opposite and saw no chinks.

"My offer," he said, "would have been paid in 14 days and would have been confidential. Are you sure…" he said looking straight at Judy, his blue eyes seeking to penetrate the mask, but unable to achieve eye contact.

"We are sure" said Max, "how long will you need to take instructions?"

Max sensed the problem he faced in that he could not indicate he was going back to talk with *Lemon* and so would have to withdraw quietly. He asked for ten minutes and invited Helen to join them. Helen agreed, and they met quietly back in Box 21. Mohammed was almost gleeful.

"Look," he began again in his now characteristic style, "If we can get away from this paying less than £400,000 ourselves that is one hell of a result. Freddie – I appreciate your advice but let's go back to Portia and cut a deal. We can do £500,000 global and ask them to pick up say £150,000."

The meeting moved back to Box 17 and Portia, Blackberry to her ear, bidded them to wait for a moment before beckoning them in. Freddie explained that the 'bad guys' as he now termed them would take £480,000 plus costs but might go under in his view. He wondered at £500,000 global.

Portia looked at her team. She had authority and saw the wisdom in that: but stuck to her guns. £100,000 was her contribution. Max suggested that 40% of the settlement sum was a fine deal and suddenly Portia tensed.

Helen again having been quiet for a while, now leant forward.

"If this went to Court could either of you tell me how long it might take, and what the costs would be – and how publicity might come into play?"

Instead of the expected reply, Portia said quietly "£150,000: final offer, no publicity at all. *Lemon* to pay *Three Tigers* directly in 7 days as consultancy fees on our books."

Freddie looked at Graham, then Mohammed and Peter. They were all nodding, Mohammed especially trying to look grave, thought Helen. Deal.

Ten minutes later, and some three hours after the mediation began, all of the participants met back in the Jeff Astle Boardroom. Portia sat almost smiling but it was Freddie who did the talking.

Judy, Jim – thank you for coming today: we at *Three Tigers* have a final offer to make and it is global. We do not think that your claim is worth more than £450,000 but, knowing that your legal fees are what they are we are prepared to pay £500,000 to walk away, and from that you will need to pay 7 Solicitors. Now we think that means you will pick up about

£472,000 if your lawyers do not relent but as we say – that is more than fair. We will go no higher. Max?"

Helen looked at Max – who said that he anticipated this move and had instructions to accept if it was offered. Smiles did then break out around the table. Helen asked who was going to write up the deal and at that point Max produced, rather too quickly perhaps, a fully typed up heads of agreement which he handed to Portia and Freddie.

"Nothing to do with me, thanks Max" said Portia. "I just want to say how pleased I am for Jim, and Judy. On behalf of *Lemon*, the other innocent party here, we wish you both well." With the heads perused and signed, Helen declared the mediation over and thanked everyone for working with her.

They shook hands, and left.

Three months later, driving back from a successful morning of mediation in Gloucester, Helen saw a sign to Appleby. "Why not?" she thought.

She pointed her Audi A5 Coupe along the winding B-road which was well maintained and within minutes the village was in view, in all its stone and Cotswold splendour.

On the edge of the village she saw the now restored Old Bull restaurant, with a pleasant little sign declaring it to be newly opened and 'Under New Management'. "Good Honest Food" said a chalk board "Served in The Old Laundry".

Not a bad place for lunch, she thought, as she parked up. Not a bad place at all.

Index